D1575949

WE HOLD OUR BREATH

WE HOLD OUR BREATH

A JOURNEY TO TEXAS

BETWEEN STORMS

MICAH FIELDS

W. W. NORTON & COMPANY
Celebrating a Century of Independent Publishing

For information about permission to reproduce selections from this
book, write to Permissions, W. W. Norton & Company, Inc.,
500 Fifth Avenue, New York, NY 10110

For information about special discounts for bulk purchases, please
contact W. W. Norton Special Sales at specialsales@wwnorton.com
or 800-233-4830

Manufacturing by Versa Press
Book design by Brooke Koven
Production manager: Julia Druskin

ISBN 978-1-324-00379-3

W. W. Norton & Company, Inc.
500 Fifth Avenue, New York, N.Y. 10110
www.wwnorton.com

W. W. Norton & Company Ltd.
15 Carlisle Street, London W1D 3BS

1 2 3 4 5 6 7 8 9 0

CONTENTS

The literature of the city—nearly, but not all, modern literature—is panoramic, sometimes celebratory, often horror-struck: the hubbub of voices speaking different languages or dialects, the conglomeration of apprehended fragments. Its medium is the collage; its science that opposites attract; its logic that every proposition and its converse are equally true.

—ELIOT WEINBERGER

After all anybody is as their land and air is.

—GERTRUDE STEIN

Most of Houston will spend eternity in hell.

—BILLY GRAHAM

AUTHOR'S NOTE

THIS IS HOW a flood is born. It comes in sneaking increments of inches and hours. It arrives with the soft accumulation of a drizzle, innocent at first, sent down from the pent-up moisture of heaving clouds.

At first, the rain falls into a dutiful chain of events. It gathers on the shoulders of roads, shedding off windshields and roofs, forming impromptu creeks in the gutters and sidewalks. It organizes itself quietly, obeying commands as simple as gravity and slope, occupying insignificant depressions: an upturned leaf, the shallow bowl of a pothole, a dip in a driveway. Droplets absorb into grass and soil. Parched concrete holds what it can. Asphalt swells. Drains swirl. Children, loading a bus for school, carry the trivial weight of rain in their soaked clothes and hair. In a parking lot, a man's car, the sunroof left open, accepts the gift of rain onto its upholstered interior, onto its seats and plastic console. Rivulets fill the small basins of cupholders.

The reality of a flood, its basic principles, are simple. We know how they work. But the event itself challenges the imagination. The essential ingredients of a flood—the possibility of rain without end, its ability to rise and consume, the artful treachery of water—confound us. In this sense, the defining characteristic of a flood, more than any sight or sound, or smell, is surprise.

———

IT IS no secret the city was built on a foundation of mud. The errors involved are obvious, and the question of reasoning is useless, for its answer is lost in the mouths of the long dead. Instead, the most popular concern—the one that is repeated by outsiders until it has taken the form of an allegation, a condemnation, a slur—is why we stayed.

WE HOLD OUR BREATH

I

EMPIRE OF MUD

ONSIDER, FOR STARTERS, the shamelessly provoca-
tive roots of its name: a title chosen by the city's found-
ers as a strategy to garner political favor from Sam Houston,
the president of the new republic of Texas, a.k.a. *Ka'lanu*, or
"the Black Raven," to his Native American compatriots, with
whom he was close. A sour-mouthed, hard-living Virginian
who preferred following deer tracks to the pursuit of notori-
ety and fame, whose life was mired in scandal, punctuated
by salacious disputes and self-imposed exile. The former con-
gressman who once—after a heated spat on the floor of the
U.S. House of Representatives concerning legislative efforts
to secure provisions for the soon-to-be displaced nation of the
Cherokee, whom he defended—chased down and thrashed
the hind of Ohio representative William Stanbery with a
hickory cane in broad daylight on the streets of Washington. A figure the poet William Carlos Williams described

as "a man of primitive vigors," a man who "when in deep thought whittled pine sticks," and wore "tigerskin vest, blanket, sombrero, joined Baptist church, opposed secession of southern states, lived to have Lincoln recognize him by offer of a Major-Generalship, which he refused . . ."

An imposing figure for his time, at well beyond six feet, whose substantial frame commanded respect by nature of its upper features alone: his pupils frozen lagoons set beneath his gleaming bald butte of a forehead, his tight frown lodged between granite jowls, the broad prow of a nose, and his chin, slightly upturned and gracefully dimpled as if thumped, from a great distance, by an enemy musket ball.

Legend maintains he was an exacting force of rage in battle, leading his troops valiantly across the sodden plains of southeast Texas. Hobbled by a bullet-shattered ankle, he commanded his unit to defeat a rested and oversized Mexican army in eighteen minutes flat on horseback, then galloped his stallion upriver to capture the disguised and retreating president of Mexico, General Antonio López de Santa Anna, whereupon he accepted the general's surrender and sparked the subsequent bloody tumult and acquisition of land without which there would be no Nevada, no Utah or California, no *West* as we have come to know it.

He was a chronic shatterer—it was gossiped, with a fervor only glossed by blushing historians—of Victorian hearts. A shirker of tedious responsibility. A flight risk, prone to idleness and wandering in childhood. A brusque and disagreeable parent at best, entirely absent at worst. A phony Unionist and an owner of slaves. A boisterous lout in dungarees and crumpled shirts. A drunk.

Nowadays, driving from the city's center outward, cutting

a line toward Dallas on Interstate 45, you will encounter his effigy twice in one hour. First he is cast in bronze, pointing far off from his saddle, perched on a stone arch in Hermann Park. Then he is found towering roadside in Huntsville, a sixty-seven-foot mold of bone-white concrete, that menacing cane in hand. The statue is perched on a ten-foot-high granite slab, and inside Sam's colossal head a cement mixer was buried—the very machine employed to build the figure—after it "died" on the last day of construction. "A tribute to courage," the statue's dedication reads.

IT IS worth noting, before anything else, that this brazen attitude was the city's first inheritance. That the city arose from a period of conflict and national anxiety, preceded by the reputation of a remarkable, unstable man, spawned by the swollen imaginations of East Coast prospectors, disputed, won, and gouged out from the sucking bowl of a swamp, stamped and wrought into domestic submission. From this tradition of resistance—to predominant sense and judgment, and decorum, to the land itself, for better or worse—it carved its image. By pure tenacity it managed to exist. By similar measures it got its name. By plow and pavement it sustained its people. Against mud and insult it found its way.

LOOKING AT it now, in the privilege of context, it is no wonder some believe this city was a giant mistake. From a contemporary vantage, the choice to settle here does seem immediately absurd. The soil is too soft. The weather is no good. The air is thick, and the water is foul, filled with all manner of natural threats: alligators, water moccasins, tricky currents, festering bacteria, swarms of mosquitoes, putrid moats of quicksand, and on and on.

The city itself sits on a large county, and the defined borders of the county, as they were drawn up and finalized in 1838, appear arbitrary at a glance, irregularly shaped and sharp at one end, like the compressed lower half of an animal's jaw. To its west, the jaw juts into a region of dense Texas timber, and from there it stretches nearly seventy-five miles east, ending in Galveston Bay, on the Gulf of Mexico's northwestern shoulder. To the north and south, its perimeter runs parallel with the silten bottomlands of rivers that race toward the coast, carrying the dirt and rain of other states. The county's surface follows a subtle, water-bound slant, and its average elevation ranges between zero and one hundred feet above sea level. In the whole 1,777 square miles of the county of Harris, where nearly five million live, there are no significant rises or dips to speak of. It is not a place, generally, where people speak of "views."

CONFRONTED WITH this flat and dreary country in 1836, land speculator Augustus Allen's response was to lie. He knew the setting was not ideal. He knew he could not lure people—especially moneyed, urban-born settlers—to a remote swamp, situated on the tenuous frontiers of an infant republic, without some risky exaggerations. Allen—who, along with his brother John, had purchased the land, practically sight-unseen, for less than a dollar per acre—knew there were characteristics of the place that he could not change with any store of time or labor. He didn't care. He thought only of perception, and how he might manipulate it.

"When the rich lands of this country shall be settled, a trade will flow to it, making it, beyond all doubt, the greatest interior commercial emporium of Texas," wrote Allen, in August 1836, in an announcement with the *Telegraph and Texas Register*, intending to entice gullible migrants southward. His spiel continued:

> Nature seems to have designated this place for the future seat of Government. It is handsome and beautifully elevated, salubrious and well watered, and now in the very heart or centre of population, and will be so for a length of time to come . . . There is no place in Texas more healthy, having an abundance of excellent spring water, and enjoying the sea breeze in all its freshness. No place in Texas possesses so many advantages for building, having Pine, Ash, Cedar and Oak in inexhaustible quantities; also the tall and beautiful Magnolia grows in abundance. In the vicinity are fine quarries of stone.

In more accurate terms, what the Allen brothers had acquired was a wasteland. The "salubrious and well watered" qualities Augustus had touted were, in fact, a confusing network of bayous (the Southern parlance for that peculiar blend of swamp and canal, a bastardization of *bayuk*, the Choctaw word for "small stream"), characterized by sluggish, turbid currents, home to sunning gators and steep, slippery banks. The system's main artery, Buffalo Bayou, collected its sibling tributaries before trickling into the shallow, warm-water bays of the Gulf. At the time Augustus first glimpsed it, Buffalo Bayou was no more than a prominent ditch. It could hardly accommodate a dugout canoe, much less a hulking steamer loaded with freight, but it was this ditch, the Allens believed, with hefty imagination, that would link Houston to the currents of trade and transform a difficult swamp into "the greatest interior commercial emporium of Texas."

The Allens' claim also included a significant spread of soft coastal marsh blanketed by a dense, peculiar dirt, a substance heavy in clay and loam, later known as Houston Black, the official state soil—a nuisance to farmers and itinerants alike. In drought, settlers learned, the soil gave way to deep, gaping cracks across the plains. In morbid instances, the cracks were known to trap and fracture the legs of wandering cattle and horses, forming a perilous, impassable hazard. When wet, the mud halted wheeled travel, bogging the axles of wagons and carts, and in heavy rains, after it absorbed what moisture it could, the mud assumed an impervious layer—the solid bottom of an earthen bowl—flooding the vicinity. Visitors cursed the stuff. Walking proved a filthy chore. Sickness thrived in the often-stagnant pools of floodwater and marsh. The foundations of early structures sank and warped on the soft sponge of their property.

Later, in the relative privacy of his memoirs, Augustus would offer a more truthful account of his city's construction, the mud a prominent villain:

One could hardly picture the jungle and swampy sweet-gum woods that a good portion of this city is built upon. The swampy grounds had to be cleared and drained . . . The labor of clearing the great space was done by negro slaves and Mexicans, as no white man could have endured the insect bites and malaria, snake bites, impure water . . .

On the backs of those laborers and slaves, under the direction of Augustus and his comrades, the town emerged in spite of its resistant setting. From the very start, visitors slung harsh criticism at the city. They mocked the dream the Allens struggled to set in motion. In 1848, the Catholic missionary Emmanuel-Henri-Dieudonné Domenech soiled his boots in the ankle-deep slop that covered the place. In correspondence, fed up and self-righteous, he complained the settlement was "infested with Methodists and ants," and deemed it "a wretched little town composed of about twenty shops and a hundred huts, dispersed here and there, among trunks of felled trees."

In 1854, a Methodist bishop himself, James O. Andrew, would lay his own curses upon the young metropolis, prescribing it an urgent moral cleansing:

> The town, I suppose, contains some two thousand inhabi-
> tants, who are said to be friendly and hospitable. I noticed
> grog-shops in great abundance, and I fear they do a pros-
> perous business . . . Beyond all doubt, there is a great
> need for a deep, a thorough, a sweeping revival of reli-
> gion in Houston; for in addition to the usual evil influ-
> ences exerted against what is holy, they have here more
> of infidelity, subtle, organized, and boldly blasphemous,
> than I have met in any place of its size in all my journey-
> ings. May God graciously visit Houston with a mighty
> revival of religion, and that right soon!

Another early visitor, John Dancy, took his turn at more concise, secular defamation, naming Houston "one of the muddiest and most disagreeable places on earth."

More settlers arrived, befuddled at the discrepancy between the Eden they'd been promised and the forbidding land that stood before them—the land that stuck, stubbornly, between the grooves of their boots and wagon wheels. *What are we to do with this place?* they likely wondered, wading through the dense tangle of vines and "sweetgum" saplings that stretched across their parcels. *How shall I make a home so far from any?*

The first literature of Houston, then, came as insult. Its first emotion was disappointment—a mounting sense of shame for its very dirt. Stitched together, these early impressions began to write a book of the place. They formed an anthology of offenses.

Still, development pressed stubbornly on. The *Telegraph and Texas Register* soon ran another promotional bit, no doubt encouraged by Augustus, announcing the first successful navigation of Buffalo Bayou by a large vessel. On January 27, 1837, the paper boasted:

THE FACT PROVED: The steamboat Laura, captain Grayson, arrived at the city of Houston some few days since without obstruction, thus it is proved that Houston will be a port of entry.

Slowly but surely, domestication took hold. The city expanded in fits and starts. Developers dredged the bayous, broke their banks into the lots of early subdivisions, and razed the groves of magnolia that once had stood, stately and fragrant, on the territory's sprawling, humid plains. They built merchant centers and exchange posts, and a bustling wharf for the transfer of lumber and other goods. In 1837, only a year into the territory's independence and formal status as the Republic of Texas, Houston was named the capital, serving as such until the headquarters was relocated in 1839 to drier, more centralized environs, at a site on the banks of the Colorado River in modern-day Austin.

Industrial and agricultural economies gathered momentum in the city's radius, many of sinister and predatory origin. In the late years of slavery in the United States, opportunists from neighboring Southern states emigrated from their crowded parcels out east and began raising sugarcane in the nutrient-rich bottomlands of Texas. Land adjacent to major rivers and bayous was sectioned into long, slender tracts, affording each operation port access for export, water supply, and an unlimited store of dense, crimson mud—a commodity that enslaved people harvested, formed into bricks, fired, and used to construct homes and agricultural structures needed for the processing of sugarcane and cotton. These new plots mimicked the plantations of tropical colonies, where enslaved people had long labored in the sweltering brickhouse cane-boiling facilities of the Caribbean Islands. The neo-plantations of Texas were no less gruesome in their tactics of production, forcing men and women to slog day and night, hovered over scalding vats of boiled syrup, slashing cane in steaming, sun-beaten fields. Soon, in keeping with the bold promises of Augustus Allen, the remote outpost on Buffalo Bayou blossomed into a slave-dependent commercial nexus, distributing sugar and cotton throughout the South and up the East Coast.

Following abolition and its enforcement in the late nine-teenth century, Texas sugar plantations in turn gave way to a new device of slavery by another name, converting them-selves into operations run on the dubious, state-endorsed "convict leasing" program, which forced the incarcerated to take up where their ancestors had left off. So-called "farm-ers" bought land under the expectation of inheriting such labor as a cheap and renewable resource, enjoying the spoils of that same thick and lucrative mud. Again, a new breed of speculators rolled in. One 1908 real estate flier for a Houston cane-farming plot touted the city's geological good fortune, describing the soil as "superior to every region on earth for the most perfect and profitable growth of sugar cane."

Cotton thrived, too, and rice, and some cattle. Roads—merely wet ruts at first—suddenly crisscrossed the region, connecting markets, farms, and residential clusters of homes. In 1856, the Texas legislature voted to make Houston the cen-ter of the state's railroad system, beating out the neighboring port of Galveston, and a web of railroads was built, linking hubs to larger, port-bound lines. By the turn of the century, the system reached its steel tendrils into fledgling territories to the West and beyond. By 1923, the city had solidified its self-perception as a gatekeeper of commerce across the con-tinent, touting its rail clout in a promotional pamphlet as the city "where seventeen railroads meet the sea."

THE CITY spread like a glass of milk spilled on the wob-bling table of Texan plains. What formed was a town with no discernible center, no clear pattern or plan, but a frenetic, haphazard mess of settlement, unbound by neighboring cities or thorough planning of any kind. No cliffs or plunging valleys inhibited the city's sprawl. No sense of urban ethics—aside from the clean absolution of capitalism, the infinite hall pass of *opportunity*, the wide-open Southwestern frontier—dictated its shape. A new species of American metropolis emerged, by way of a scattered mess of encampments, neighborhoods, and plantations. Refineries and merchant centers sprang up alongside housing developments and agricultural plots. Meanwhile, highways snaked their way through the confusion. In the early gestures of municipal government, the city officials had voted—as they continue to do in Houston—to forgo the precautionary measures of zoning, thereby freeing the town and its people from the standard regulations of land use. The absence of zoning bred a novel chaos to the way a city might compose itself.

Generations later, scholars would compare the city's growth to that of other major urban areas, employing the simile of a living organism. Where more traditional, older towns—cities built on European models of density and walkability, the ancient sense of the urban commons, like New York and Boston—had sprouted like a thriving plant, branching out from their municipal "seeds" (downtown) into arms of boroughs and suburbs, the development of Houston unfolded as a decentralized labyrinth. It had no nucleus, obeyed no rules of physics or nature. It grew, instead, like a gigantic fungus, germinating in pockets of opportunity, dying out then migrating, exhausting the resources in one host in order to pick up and move irreverently to the next.

In time, Houston's method of expansion posed a unique and quickly intensifying problem. To be sure, the city had earned its keep, rising from the mire of skepticism and establishing its viability as a metropolis-to-be, holding more than one hundred thousand souls by 1915, more than five hundred thousand by 1950, and well beyond a million by 1969, the same year its name—along with that weighty legacy it bore—became the first word to be spoken from the surface of the moon, its prominence beamed into expectant living rooms across the nation. Heralded as "Space City" for its pioneering role in lunar exploration, Houston simultaneously became a purveyor of another kind of space, inflating itself to accommodate a patchwork of mini cities within a giant one, swallowing up the dense marsh and forests that once had resisted its emergence.

But the bare evidence of its population cannot sustain a city. It is not the size of the place that matters, exclusively, nor is it the question of whether its inhabitants can simply *fit*. Now its dilemma was an existential one. Its future was an environmental equation. As the rate of development multiplied, and pads of concrete and houses took over from where water had once stood, the simple issue of feasibility was gone. The city's possibility was no longer a measure of the human ability to buy into the dream, to move there, and build. It was a concern, rather, of geological perspective, and the limits of land itself.

2

THE ARMS OF GOD

AQUICK RECKONING OF inundation and all its forms: The iterations of Earth's floods can be broken into a few distinct categories. Some floods require rain; others, the whims of isolated bodies of water—the slow but dreadful overflow of dams and levees, the redirection of creeks and rivers, and the swelling of bays. Mercurial and diverse, floods come both instantly and over millennia, arriving on our porch in trivial puddles and in global and fearsome scale. To regard them is science and art, the subject of our most poetic and biblical metaphors. Floods are curses and cleansings, the stuff of cathartic absolution and righteous punishment. Today, the most common floods are given names. There are *storm surges*—a flood brought on by the momentum of an advancing hurricane, a devastating wall of water shoved across the land. There are *flash floods* and *river floods*, which carry their ingredients in their names, and there are *surface floods*, a species that spreads languidly across the land, usually initiated by sustained rain on an area covered in concrete or other impermeable substance, such as the tightly grouped roofs of homes and other buildings, the hard-packed soil of soccer fields and lawns. All floods possess the potential for immeasurable destruction, and each strain of disaster brings with it a string of appropriate reactions. An exhaustive list compiled by the National Oceanic and Atmospheric Administration's National Severe Storms Laboratory includes commands alongside illustrated descriptions of each flood's behavior. The images are simple, cartoonish, not unlike the graphics in an airplane's evacuation manual. *Find high ground*, one installment says. *Stay where you are*, says another. *Retreat inland. Seek flotation.* Victims of each flood, the guide argues, confront a series of choices for survival, the tactics of which vary widely based on conditions. The resource inspires peace of mind, if only in its sterile organization, offering the promise that by pure ingenuity and preparedness one might reign over the worst instance of nature. Confronted with the isolated occurrence of one of these floods, the advantage is preparedness, education, calm. In the event of all four at once, however, there exists no feasible strategy, no textbook procedure for evacuation and evasion—no clear hope, in other words.

———

It was the animals that got to me first. It was the swift and anomalous conduct of wildlife, the ants in particular, which were observed floating in odd heaps throughout the city, each insect clasped to one another, thousands of them, like some kind of freakish, buoyant phalanx. They drifted, impermeable and furious, for miles. Sources warned residents to stay away—the rafts of displaced colonies might swarm your body in an instant, biting on instinct. In the late summer of 2017, an Ohio-sized wheel of a storm swung over the Gulf, parked itself atop the city, and dumped several feet of steady rainfall. I'd watched the first progress of the storm from my home in the Midwest, more than a thousand miles from the hurricane's landfall. In the hours that followed, an unprecedented flood took shape on the entire Texas coast, concentrating in the city of Houston. Overwhelmed by runoff, major drainage channels seized, the bayous breached, and the place transformed into an ever-deepening basin.

The weather had turned the terrain strange, and the animals seemed to channel its most dramatic permutations. Whole prairie and riparian habitats clashed. At one point in the days following the storm, driving between road blockages that had been repurposed as boat ramps, I spotted three deer in a quarter-mile stretch of suspended freeway, all of them dead, all of them mature bucks, there on the damp shoulder high above the city, improbably posed like grotesque taxidermy. Cattle, too, and horses, still alive but desperate, were huddled on bare islands of pasture, and I began to think, in an irrational spiral of anxiety, that the rain would never stop, that the fauna would disappear, that the weight of the flood would keep pushing, and the city I knew as a child would sink, quietly, gradually, into an industrial Atlantis. For more than a month, I stayed on alert, electrified by faint paranoia.

STILL AT my home in Iowa, I'd monitored the weather radar and watched Hurricane Harvey blossom into a fierce, twirling rose over the Gulf. When the eye got closer to Texas, I turned to the feed of a webcam in Corpus Christi, monitoring the southern half of the state's coast. Before evacuating, a man had propped his laptop in the kitchen, turned it toward an east-facing window, and left it on. The stream lasted until the sky sank and the rains turned horizontal. The shrubs began to whip back and curl over the home's deck. Then the feed went black. I switched to another live cam, this time on a dock in Port O'Connor, farther up the coastline, where a row of skiffs bobbed, then rocked, then shanked violently against their pilings. The storm was grinding north. When the video feed in Port O'Connor dropped, I called my mother. She lives in far west Houston, in a two-story house looking out over the upper reaches of Buffalo Bayou and the Brazos River. Just a year before she'd watched the bayou crest and swallow a home behind hers. I called once, and she didn't answer. Then I tried again, and again. Finally she picked up, and she sounded calm. The storm was still distant, making its ominous U-turn back toward Bay City, lining up for its projected recharge on the coast. My mother was getting her nails done.

The stores had been a mess, she said, and she'd avoided the quarrels over cases of Aquafina, grabbing only minor provisions: Pop-Tarts and a case of sparkling water. She'd grown up in this place, raised me there, and she'd learned, like millions of other coastal residents, how to survive the omnipresent threats of inundation, how to shrug off the Gulf's seasonal proddings. If Harvey was the storm they said it was, she decided, she'd accept it with a local's casual grace. She'd face it with fortitude and French tips. She went to sleep when the rain came, and hours later she woke to a knock at the door. A team in an airboat had floated up to her porch. They told her it was time to leave. The bayou was still rising. The house was surrounded by a chocolate-brown moat of churning floodwater. She thought of her pets, of the furniture, and of the calm, durable poise with which she'd approached every storm's taunt until then. She stayed.

"Where's the water?" I began texting her every half hour.

"Still up," she kept replying.

———

I CALLED Nigel, a friend from the Marines I hadn't seen in years, and asked if he'd help drive the last stretch down to my mother. He had a boat, and a jacked-up Jeep, and he lived halfway to Houston, in Tulsa, with his girlfriend and a restless Weimaraner. That weekend he'd made plans to be on calmer waters, relaxing, drinking beer and dunking blood-soaked treble hooks into the catfish holes of Tenkiller Lake. But the storm insisted otherwise.

I made it to Oklahoma that night, clipping south across the mostly empty, two-lane highways, the radio off and the windows down. When I got to Tulsa, Nigel was up and ready at the door. He'd brewed a pot of coffee, stuffed a bag with beef jerky and a change of clothes, and hitched up his boat—a small aluminum craft, dented but sturdy, with a tiller outboard motor and a mess of trotlines tangled in the bow. Inside, Nigel's girlfriend was still up, perched listlessly on the couch with the dog coiled against her leg, a muted episode of *House Hunters* unfolding on the TV.

I left my car in the driveway, and from there we took off, bouncing over the Jeep's roaring mud tires until Houston glowed in the distance. The air thickened with each hour as we moved closer to the Gulf. A light rain came first, soon intensifying to a downpour, the Jeep's wipers a flashing blur. Then, without warning, a string of barricades appeared, blocking the road. Just beyond them, the highway dipped into a false shore. We'd reached the limit of Interstate 45 as soon as we crossed the Harris County line. The eye had hit on Saturday, and the city had gone under by Monday. It was Tuesday, both of us groggy and sore-eyed, as I helped Nigel back the boat's trailer into a makeshift launch in the parking lot of a Best Buy.

I didn't know what I'd do for my mother. Chances were I couldn't reach her. But I felt a pull in my gut, some cocktail of love and guilt. I felt that ethically slippery urge to *bear witness*, which is not without its selfish drive to inhabit an experience one can't stand to observe from a distance. I wanted to be inside that flood, inside my city. I wanted to hurt along with it.

In the past few years, following a series of moves and personal crises, some self-inflicted and others not, I'd grown into feeling constantly shaken and displaced, uprooted and reaching for the familiar image of home—the amorphous swath of East Texas where I'd grown up—for the particular grit and grain of its land and people, its humid swath of pine and oak, its beaches, its inescapable heat and highways, and, of course, its city. In the comfort of emotional and physical distance, before the storm, I'd had the privilege of ambivalence, of a wavering, fair-weather allegiance. But the storm, it seemed, had unlocked a spell of sudden and lucid conviction.

When the water started to rise, I was forced to make a choice, and quickly: to stay back, retreating into an identity more and more obscured, letting the place fade from my memory, or to go, *now*. Before Nigel offered to help, I'd committed to the desperate, illogical, and solitary plan of driving my rented sedan into the city, traveling until the floodwater—carrying with it a sea of evicted ants and debris—reached the windows. I'd make a drastic ceremony of it. I'd ditch the car, then get out and wade, then swim. I'd keep moving with each strange new current, struggling until I reached the city's heart, wherever it was. In that place, I fantasized, in the lowest depths of the flood, under the streets and homes, held in place by a world of pressure, was a massive, stoppered drain, with a plug as simple as a sink's. I'd reach out, in a lunge of frustration, toward that dark, concentrated pit of the city, grab hold of some lingering, psychic chain, and pull it.

———

THERE WAS once order here. The first people to inhabit this place—a tribe unique to the Gulf Coast known as the Karankawa—understood and respected the region's seasonal rhythms. The memory of their existence, while faint and forcibly suppressed, casts harsh light on our own stubborn naivete. Their stories, which live underneath us, pressed between sand and rock, reflect a picture of the land as it was meant to be.

When the Spanish encountered the Karankawa for the first time in the sixteenth century, their journals noted the imposing height of the tribe's members (most of whom stood over five feet seven inches, much taller than the average European), and the team of explorers made hasty presumptions about the Karankawas' innate hostility. They gawked at the women, speculated that their tattoos had aggressive meanings, and portrayed the tribe's rituals as demonic and perverse. Ultimately displaced by violence at the hands of reckless and paranoid settlers who arrived in the late nineteenth century to establish small ranches on the coast, the Karankawa were often described and villainized as fierce and simple giants, dismissed by whites as shiftless wanderers. But the nomadic tribe had moved as the weather moved, with precise intuition. They had spent their summers on the shore, when the weather was mild and the fishing lucrative, then migrated inland and westward during the fall and winter, sheltering in the protective pine forests and oak stands of the innermost coastal plains.

In the calmer seasons of spring and summer, the tribe's families had thrived on the abundant food source of estuaries and bays, stalking speckled trout and flounder in the tide marshes and flats, burning driftwood fires in the sand near their dwellings made of tanned hides. Skillful hunters, they had crouched underneath thin spears behind cruising schools of redfish, stealthily navigating the clusters of mangroves, their bodies covered with the macerated fat of sharks—a natural mosquito repellent. Archaeological research and the rare fragments of oral histories inform us that the Karankawa, contrary to Eurocentric lore, did not practice cannibalism, but instead existed in relative amity with most neighboring tribes, were proficient traders, and spoke a language peculiarly isolated from that of most indigenous North American tribes. They made remarkable art from pigments and clay not seen among other early Gulf Coast peoples, and they regularly practiced elaborate spiritual ceremonies heightened by the consumption of "black drink," an elixir made of roasted and boiled holly leaves. Their behavior and physiology (and even the unique markings found on fragments of their pottery and other crafts, some say) more closely resembled those of tribes from the Caribbean and the Middle East, a correlation suggesting the Karankawa, for reasons that remain mysterious, once made an enormous, transoceanic journey to land here, on the beaches that give way to the sodden marsh and prairie of present-day Houston.

Vast migration, it seemed, was endemic. The Karankawa lexicon, for instance, claims three different variations for "crane," the elegant, towering bird and master of flighted migrants (North American varieties, both whooping cranes and sandhills, still land in the wetlands of east Texas each November—albeit in dwindling, precious numbers—after a flight from their summering grounds in Canada's Northwest Territories). In the Karankawas' annual exodus from the coast, while the bays received their regular beatings from storms and disastrous surges, they would have followed the route of the crane in reverse, no doubt glimpsing the bird in their cruising flocks of thousands. The cranes can float for miles on a single heave of their wings. Preyed upon in the nineteenth century for their stylish plumes, whooping cranes eventually met their demise as the Karankawa did, shot down en masse by European settlers. By the 1940s, fewer than fifty whooping cranes existed in the wild, and today they survive only in closely monitored families, their population rebounding to scarcely more than three hundred. The remaining number of Karankawa tribal members on the coast, however, remains a mystery.

WITHOUT PERMISSION or warning, in the forceful lilt of their European tongues, early Spanish explorers began by laying new titles upon the land. Not long after their first encounters with the Karankawa, they gave one of Texas's longest rivers a Christian name to mark its brutal current: *Brazos de Dios*. The Arms of God.

For centuries before European colonization, the Karankawa traced the circuitous banks of the Brazos River on their travels inland. Methods of subsistence shifted as the dunes and mangroves gave way to a landscape of scraggly mesquite; a seafood diet was replaced by a steady menu of deer and hares. The Spanish cast a more exploitative eye toward the river. To those early, would-be conquerors, the Brazos— which drains much of northern and coastal Texas, its headwaters gathering far in the highlands of New Mexico and winding for more than eight hundred miles before emptying into its brackish mouth at the Gulf of Mexico—symbolized the land's potential for unknown riches, as well as the swift means by which travelers might reach them.

Much to the Spaniards' disappointment, however, the Brazos held no gold, and its assumed navigability proved false. Its shifting banks provided no reliable earth for encampment. Its muddy depths hid hazardous snags, sandbars, and eddies, and its route took on a frustratingly indirect path through the treasureless wilderness, like a writhing, dirty snake, into the continent's unforgiving drylands.

Instead of carrying them to fame and fortune, the mouth of the Brazos became a treacherous gate to the region, especially for one early Spaniard, the accidental explorer Álvar Núñez Cabeza de Vaca, whose team of sailors wrecked a makeshift barge onto present-day Galveston in 1528. Destitute and stranded, they cursed the island before they even stood on it. They sat for days beyond the breakers, draped over the broken timber of their raft, feasting on spoiled rations of corn and meat from their slaughtered horses. After the fate they saw there, they named the place *Isla Malhado*, Isle of Misfortune, and when they finally reached the shore they began a long and hopeless trek westward.

"No service is left to me but to bring an account to Your Majesty of the nine years I wandered through many very strange lands, lost and naked," writes Cabeza de Vaca in the beginning of *La Relación*, the narrative that documents his travels through the unmapped hills.

To save his own flesh, Cabeza de Vaca often lied. He posed as a healer, laying his hands on the skin of pained tribespeople in coordinates no European man had set foot on before. He removed arrows lodged in the chests of warriors. He starved, nearly died of thirst, and feasted on prickly pear and the hearts of deer.

"They eat earth and wood," he wrote of the indigenous people he confronted. When taken in by a tribe, he observed, repulsed, the sight of "a man married to another." His body broke. "We shed our skin twice a year, like snakes," he wrote, presumably during a first encounter with sunburn, in the scorching plains of West Texas.

La Relación constituted the territory's first memoir, a wild document, poetic and full of death, rambling and ignorant. It is the dispatch of a young man with no certain future, at times enslaved by the indigenous peoples he encountered, at other times worshipped. His route wound a desperate loop through the desert from which he eventually returned, dressed in the skins of animals, gaunt and shaken. His team, dwindling in number each year, covered thousands of miles as they trudged through what would become the borderlands of Texas and Mexico. But first they had to cross the Brazos, and the river remained the reference from which they understood their entire world thereafter.

Though bridled by a sequence of dams now, harnessed for power and recreation in intermittent reservoirs strung across Texas, the wrath of the Brazos's current remains an imposing feature of the landscape. It gushes past the city of Houston, forming its jagged, southwestern border, a vein of wilderness cutting through the suburbs. When viewed from above, the Brazos's channels resemble the braided arms of a giant—the sprawled-out limbs of a god—opaque with silt, laced with the sinew of battling currents, its boils of undertow and suction mingling on the surface. The river still floods and changes course as it pleases, eroding its banks into high cliffs, swallowing fallen trees and rotting docks, and, on occasion, sweeping away entire homes caught in its path. Savvy anglers know the bounty it holds. Armed with ranks of poles, trot-lines, and jugs, they pursue the massive catfish and gar lingering deep in its eddies, but their attempts are unsuccessful more often than not. Fishing for deep-dwelling species, they catch their hooks instead on sunken debris, tangling their line in the endless flotsam spilling downstream, their costly lures and sinkers sucked into feet of mud.

Over time, the river's immediate vicinity has given way to human neglect, known to attract the itinerant and outcast. Worried citizens claim crimes abound in the tucked-away shadows underneath bridges and trestles. Closer to the city, on unclaimed patches of ground below the river's high-water mark, clusters of tents and strung-up tarps appear seemingly overnight, forming makeshift towns, harboring those literally on the fringe. Increasingly, wealthier residents—

commuters who are forced to see the Brazos on the way home to their gated communities of garish stucco homes—consider the river an eyesore. From the comfortable remove of their cars, they bemoan the abundant trash that seems to gravitate toward the Brazos, the rusted-out appliances, beer cans, and bald tires that litter its muddy beaches. Their complaints cast its domain as unsightly and embarrassing, but the romantics among us still find an improbable beauty in the Brazos. There is a rare charm in its obstinance, an allure in its refusal— after generations have attempted to tame and straighten it— to simply *behave*.

———

IN THE home where she lives now, near the Brazos and the bayous that feed into it, my mother collects animals. The feral cats and dogs wander up from the water, emaciated and skit-tish, forever multiplying. My mother sprinkles trails of food to lure them in, gains their trust, and makes homes for her rescues in every room, erecting scratching posts and stacking bed linens for her salvaged family—pallets made of towels, sheets, and quilts. She builds small towns for the animals, intricate architectures of cardboard and carpet. Dyed feath-ers hang from springs on the miniature ceilings. Hardened pig's ears for the dogs. The adopted cats lounge on counters, piss in the laundry, wreck the furniture, and shred patches of sheetrock and plaster from the walls. The dogs obey their own rule of law, somehow immune to any kind of scorn or discipline. They lope through each room, their coats rotten with mange, their eyes fogged by cataracts. They gnaw on shoes and clothes, raid plates for leftover food.

Still, my mother, a fierce and restless woman, weathered by a lifetime of men and work, finds solace in the endless task of her generosity. She adores the animals, and she assigns them ornate, dignified names: Isaiah, Meredith, Brutus, Rose, Carmelita. She feeds the families of opossums when they dare to approach the porch, and she protects the armadillos that waddle, blind and awkward, through the mulch of flower beds. She takes comfort, as she always has, in the companionship of her own feral kin. Welcoming without restraint, she reigns over a kingdom of strays.

———

Like most Houstonians today, I was raised in a neighborhood that sprouted around the industrial port the Allen brothers first fantasized. I came up as a product of the drab and invasive mass of the American suburbs. There, on the ever-expanding outskirts of Houston, the Brazos at my back, I grew accustomed to the feeling of being pinned between a sprawling and fractured history.

As a child without siblings, often alone and curious, I'd venture out into the natural areas surrounding my home, exploring the scraps of wilderness that bordered our young neighborhood. I'd sneak under barbed-wire fences, committing minor trespasses, building forts, and scrawling maps of game trails, stock ponds, and the confluences of creeks. Mysteries lived in those thinning woods, and I encountered them in the haunting juxtaposition of relics and my contemporary urban existence. Sometimes, after floods, when the Brazos swelled and dropped, taking inches of topsoil with it, the past emerged. Graveyards, unregistered and neglected, poked up.

These burial plots—likely holding the bodies of former slaves and postbellum, imprisoned laborers—lingered on the fringes of baseball fields and strip malls, the crude grave markers soon to be demolished by bulldozers, and the ground slathered with a grid of concrete foundations. On the random lots of developers and holdout ranchers, tucked throughout the city, the ruins of sugar plantations lay scattered, their chunks of iron and brick jutting up from the mud. The vestiges of that economy stuck around, and syrup cauldrons once used for boiling crushed stalks of cane rusted in thickets of blackberry bushes. These working agricultural prisons still line the Brazos, and the region's oldest standing homes still contain chimneys and cisterns of bricks made from the hard-packed crimson soil of Brazos bottomland. Restless and irreverent, wandering and killing time after school, I'd dig up shards of those forgotten structures that waited in the undeveloped quadrants of neighborhoods. I found them in shallow burials, the ghosts of homes, their bricks sketching the outlines of antebellum floorplans. I skipped their fragments across ponds. The bricks stained my palms red.

Meanwhile, oil rigs, their machinery anchored deep and alone in remote corners of properties, clanked and banged during the night.

———

THE SUMMER before I entered first grade, my family purchased a small home among other houses that had been built quickly in the 1980s. The development was constructed following the wave of expansion spurred by the previous decade's financial boom, when the city's perimeter was blasted open by thriving industry, its residents liberated by cheap automobiles and a sense of endless suburban frontier. The homes in our neighborhood, bunched in tight grids and stamped from a limited number of prefabricated designs, were marketed to young, mobile families on a budget. Each model differed only slightly from the patterned proportions of another, and to look down the street was to recognize a winding rank of near-clones. The houses were made of dark brick and cement siding and sat close together on streets named for the ephemera of the Civil War. Few of the neighborhood's residents were white, while the neighborhood's street signs (Vicksburg Boulevard, Confederate Court, Bedford Forrest Drive, and the like) hung like cruel, anachronistic jokes. The street names were a product of the developers' pathetic stabs at nostalgia, a gesture toward a lost and imagined antebellum inheritance that attempted to fabricate a sensation of *oldness*.

But the homes and their streets, of course, were anything but old. Any history that did exist had been plowed from underneath in preparation for a fresh layer of occupation, and the development wore the unmistakable gleam of the new. In my child-sized palm, I could encircle an entire trunk of the cheap ash saplings that dotted the neighborhood's lawns in precise intervals. Our front curbs and sidewalks bore the crisp, jagged edges of freshly dried concrete, and you could still spot the suspiciously uneven seams in our lawns, the faint perforations where the sod had been scalped from distant fields, piled onto pallets and into trucks, and puzzle-pieced together around our foundations. No hitching posts, servants' quarters, or grand architectural features graced our properties, and no cohesive or dignified "style" clung to our facades. The homes were not Colonial or Victorian, or Modern, or any fashionable motif of the sort, but, rather, an irreverent mashup of many half-baked aesthetic traditions, meant to imply a generic pastiche of class, a hint of lavish yet affordable taste.

But the people who purchased these homes had no time for taste. Ambitious and ruthlessly practical, wrought from the hardy ethic of immigrants, they did not care to bother with elaborate décor or gentility. My family and the people we called our neighbors, the people we grew to trust and cherish—the people who, like us, pulled their cars responsibly into their driveways at six each evening, who watched the news by the synchronized firelight of their televisions every night, who traced fresh lines in the grass with their sputtering mowers each Saturday, who dumped boxes of pasta in pots of boiling water on their kitchen stovetops, who made babies between the thin sheetrock of their bedrooms, who loved and fought and grieved in their homes, both together and alone—did not care about the past. Their eyes were fixed on a wealth and security their parents did not know. For all of us, this meant the constant obliging of the contemporary. It meant participating in a fresh momentum that eschewed the clumsy accessories of nostalgia and tradition, engaging in neither the cult of "new money" nor the easy spoils of the old, but an abstract and blander sense of stability in between. It meant developing the utilitarian skill of resisting sentimentality, of not looking back, and not pausing to dwell on the complex associations attached to the land we inhabited. It meant adopting a cheaper and more pliable architecture of forgetting. In this way, the landscape of my childhood was sterile. This sterility, however, was only a placeholder for the real culture that swirled around and beneath us. To my ears as a child, this culture was drowned out by the American urge, quite literally, to bleach the world into sameness, to smear whiteness like stucco over the more nuanced lattice-work of our world.

The writer Joan Didion once contrasted the California of her youth against her travels throughout rural Alabama and Mississippi, musing on the United States's complicated relationship with its past. "In the South," she writes, "they are convinced that they have bloodied their place with history."

"In the West," she goes on, "we do not believe that anything we do can bloody the land, or change it, or touch it. How could it have come to this?"

Didion was a thinker in search of geographical resonance, constantly looking backward and forward for clues to understanding herself in relation to the land and culture of the moment. Her writing grows restless, breathless in its inquiry: "I am trying to place myself in history," she writes, announces. "I have been looking all my life for history and have yet to find it."

I spent my childhood searching, similarly, for the link between myself and the gauzy figments of history as they floated into and out of my vision: the haunting reminders of slavery's domain in my backyard, the ever-present totems of oil and extraction, the relentless growth of the city and its structures, the blithe stupidity of the names on my street's signs, and on and on. Growing up, my particular strain of the South—equal parts urban and rural, both expanding and static, wild and tamed—was not the syrupy, genteel kind that the movies portray. Nor was it the ambitious model of commercial success it aspired to be. It was a land of opposites banging against one another at every turn, a raw and painful

American collage. It presented no easy narrative or through-line, as no real person or country ever does. As a child of this place, I have been trying all my life to place myself in history. I have been looking—under rocks and buildings, under the city, in the lasting stories of the soil—for the right thread to pull, the one attached to me, sewn deep in my chest. I have yet to find it.

———

THE GROWTH of our neighborhoods did not come without painful consequence. Day in and day out, we lived with constant reminders of the environment our existence pushed up against. Stunned by our encroaching domestic behemoth, resident wildlife could not keep up, and animals struggled to adapt to life alongside us, their new and disruptive neighbors. Confused deer, robbed of their sanctuary, wandered the place, chomping at hedges and fruit-bearing trees, their graceful necks stretched up to snatch at dangling limbs. Armadillos, opossums, and pot-bellied raccoons roamed the streets at night in large squads, rich on our trash, their eyes shining like fluorescent moons when caught in headlights. Stray dogs, abandoned by families whose homes had been recently foreclosed during the building recession of the 2000s, cruised in ghostly packs, their hair matted, their collars frayed or missing. Feral and quarrelsome, they toyed with their tamed cousins—our pets—who were chained up in yards, growling through gaps in fence posts.

Alligators, too, most of their wetlands drained and packed over with gravel, found new homes in the ditches and dyed-blue ponds ornamenting suburban backyards. Occasionally, construction crews discovered them holed up in the culverts beside new developments, and when a family's beloved dog or cat disappeared, the alligators were predictably implicated. Though the claims were never confirmed, the creatures served as a convenient evil, lurking obstinately in the corners of habitat we'd yet to tame. Wary, we moved to and from our homes with faint caution and intrigue, sometimes glimpsing the ominous bulge of their leathery heads, their eyes trained on the procession of our cars and bicycles, never blinking.

Once, a neighboring group of older boys—oblivious teenagers, ruled by pubescent aggression—captured an adolescent gator near a flooding storm drain. They wrangled the animal, dragged its writhing body into a quiet cul-de-sac, and doused it with gasoline. One boy lit and tossed a match. Together they watched, faces aglow, as the animal flailed to its death.

Neighborhood parents were slow to respond. What sort of justice, they deliberated, if any, could be enacted on the boys? What punishment would properly scorn the children they'd raised into young men that suddenly so frightened and disgusted them? Their lasting silence, it seemed, was as much of an implication as any. In time, the site was cleared, the remains discarded. A charred silhouette of the animal was left behind, its memory persisting in asphalt. The site became a stinking mark of shame for the neighborhood, a small monument for the inexplicable crime that was, by some sideways logic laced with truth, the fault of our community as a whole. Together we pushed the image to the backs of our brains in an attempt to distance ourselves and to forget the sin entirely. Eventually, the gentle patterns of our place resumed. The cars returned each evening, hauling their passengers back from work and school, parking over the small, dark splotches of leaked oil in their driveways. On Saturday the mowers carved neat stripes into their seas of grass. The smell of dinner, rising from each kitchen, filled the air with competing aromas of broccoli-and-rice casseroles, curries, Vietnamese pho, simmered oxtail, and grilled asparagus sizzling in foil. Day-to-day interactions assumed the quiet veneer of normalcy, but secretly we knew, from then on, that our perspective had been drastically reconfigured. We waged the battle of suppressing—consciously or not—the admission that we, too, in a way, were the threat. We were the hideous and volatile creatures to avoid. We were the displaced and violent animals, cornering ourselves, stretching into the awkward new skins of our homes.

3

DEEP WATER

O N THE WAY into the city with Nigel, the Jeep's wipers smacked against the margins of the windshield. Through sheets of rain, we strained to follow the road's guiding yellow centerline. The sun had risen, but the weather made its exact location in the sky unclear. Only a faint, yellow bruise of light shone through the low clouds as we approached the flood.

Fatigued and hungry, we stopped at the only flickering OPEN sign we'd seen for miles, a donut shop in Spring, wedged between strip-mall storefronts. The parking lot was packed with vehicles. Inside, the place functioned as an unofficial outpost. The owner had stayed open all week, serving coffee and kolaches to neighbors and first responders cut off by the storm. Strangers shared tables and watched updates on the small television mounted above the coolers. A group of older men sat in one corner, each of them clutching a steaming Styrofoam cup. The wall behind them was covered in novelty signs, the most colorful of which read "Old Fart Xing," and below, a flip calendar remained stuck on the previous month of July, its image of a sunlit Utah canyon. Snapshots of fishermen grasping swollen bass and catfish filled the wall's tableau.

The room was alive with chatter, backed by the rhythmic metal clank of the cash register. The air was thick with the smell of hot grease. It was my first glimpse of the city's storm-rattled social atmosphere, and I'd expected a tense scene. Instead, the shop was a buzzing reunion: regulars propped in their chairs, kids knocking back chocolate milk, and troopers wrapped in their neon dusters, haggard from shifts on the barricades.

There in the donut shop, watching the coverage of the past few days, my understanding of the hurricane's wrath shifted. Until then I'd considered the devastation an isolated villain, as if it contained an identifiable, damnable nucleus. I'd imagined the flood an evil bubble of mercury plopped onto the coast, but I was wrong. Nature is not so simple. A flood doesn't distribute itself into familiarities. Its edges stretch and shrink, and Houston lay underneath its giant, erratic web, not a single sea but a multitude of individual ones.

I'd been monitoring the search-and-rescue radio chatter via app since Dallas. I'd listened to it chirp requests for rescues through the night. Each transmission came with a sense of mounting urgency, squawking loudly from the speaker of my phone. In one crackled, desperate-sounding missive, a woman rattled off the medications prescribed to her husband, who was stuck in a third-floor apartment, woozy from a recent surgery, hungry and immobile. His supplies were scarce, the woman said, and he didn't have much time. Another dispatch came from a father and his family of four. They were huddled on their roof, bracing against their chimney in the wind and rain. The water was rising. Another report came from a woman who was safe but searching for her cat, an elderly tabby named Penelope. Each message came with its own string of addresses and directions, and I'd written down a dozen or so from the night spent listening to the app, sketching out possible routes to their locations while coordinating with other volunteers. Some were close enough for us to reach, if the roads permitted. At a certain point, my fingers grew tired, and the effort seemed futile. I let the radio traffic wash over me, already exhausted and overwhelmed. Most of the distressed, I'd soon learn, were trapped within the strange maze of the flood, inaccessible by boat or on foot. They were each a stranded island in the city's archipelago, surrounded by intermittent stretches of dry and submerged land. To simply *float* to them, in most instances, was impossible.

After scarfing down two donuts each, Nigel and I took our coffees and left, feeling replenished but daunted. Heading in the direction of the flood, we zigzagged through side streets in the Jeep, approaching the city from the north, skirting west, then cutting east on an obscure two-lane. A series of barricades and washed-out bridges made progress difficult, but eventually we broke through the flood's perimeter and into the sodden heart of the city. When we got close to one of the addresses from my notebook, we pulled over at a semi-elevated spot near a cluster of box stores, parking among a small crown of fellow boaters, reporters, and cops. There, under the steady rain, we changed into boots, backed the trailer into the water, and prepped the boat for launch.

At the edge of the flood, plotting our route, we waited in a congested line of trucks, trailers, and boats owned by hunters and fishermen from all over. They'd come to Houston in the gear they had, the clothes that best suited the job, dressed in camouflage coveralls, bucket hats, and rain slickers. One by one, they slid their vessels—shallow-water fishing skiffs and dented jon boats, many of their hulls spray-painted with tableaus of homemade camo, hand-stenciled outlines of leaves and stumps—into the overflowing ditches. Many of the boaters had driven from small, bayou-adjacent towns in Louisiana, calling themselves the Cajun Navy. The national media latched on to the moniker, featuring shots of the traffic lines stretching across Lake Pontchartrain and the Atchafalaya River. News segments included shots that swept across the miles-long daisy-chain of idling trucks and their boats. The voyage of the volunteers inspired hope in Houston. The note of generosity kept ringing—embodied in people who steadily came, ready and willing, with no particular stake in the matter, to simply and instinctually *help*. On this day and many after, in the swamped parking lot of Best Buy, far from their own homes, the volunteers swapped reports and wrung the water from their clothes, heading immediately back after hauling loads of rescued Houstonians in their boats. In the background you could hear the murmur of their work reaching up through the rain. Throughout the streets and alleys erupted an orchestra of the boats' small, gurgling motors.

I LEARNED things about neighborhoods I never planned to. First: they are never flat. Even if the land they were built on resembled the level sameness of the plains, the roads slant, and the homes perch on elevated foundations. They are built to drain. In Nigel's small boat, separated from the murky and oil-streaked floodwaters by a skin of thin aluminum, I saw streets that had taken so much water they could no longer displace it. We traversed those residential lagoons, moving past the shores of lawns and garages.

Nigel did his best to guide us along medians and sidewalks, but the flooding had reached a precarious level: too high to wade, and too low to run a motor. The prop dug into the concrete. The hull knocked us into a railroad track. Nigel sat in the stern, his fist wrapped tight around the outboard motor's throttle. With each twist and flick of his wrist, he trolled us carefully over the submerged hazards of mailboxes and fire hydrants, but occasionally a loud clank would send us heaving forward, grasping for the boat's gunwales. Confronted with dead ends, we trailered the boat to the Jeep and drove, instead, in the direction of the Addicks Reservoir, the city's enormous bathtub, set to overflow in hours.

In calmer weather, under regular rainfall, Addicks Reservoir served as a fail-safe that supported a variety of inner-city recreation. The acreage encompassed a wide, concave expanse of grass and thickets, replete with a dog park, hiking trails, and a shooting range whose targets abutted the reservoir's earthen dam. Positioned at a lower elevation than the rest of the city, the reservoir began filling rapidly after Harvey made landfall, as it was designed to do, taking on the bayou's overflow and funneling it through a regulated spillway. In the mounting hours and days of rain, however, the reservoir had reached its limits. The levees had nearly crested, and the paradox of flow regulation had become obvious: crank open the gates, allowing the reservoir to drain, saving homes from flooding upstream, or dam the flows above downtown, mitigating further danger downriver. In an attempt to split the difference, the city continued to allow water through the reservoir's spillway at moderate rates, but the trickle was scarcely effective at controlling the level of water filling the reservoir. The incessant rain caused the whole drainage to continue to swell, inching westward. Neighborhoods surrounding Addicks Reservoir had flooded first, followed by a chain reaction of flooding above the reservoir, along Buffalo Bayou. At the bayou's upper end was my mother's home, along with thousands of others, and the storm had already begun to claim the lowest-lying structures. The real danger to come, sources claimed, was the eventual breach of Addicks Reservoir in its entirety, whereupon residents yet to evacuate, like my mother—the ones who simply refused or were unable to escape—would be overcome by the advancing wall of water.

Nigel and I wound through the maze of barricades, avoiding flooded bridges, until we could no longer push through the water in the Jeep. On the perimeter of a neighborhood where we parked and dismounted, we met a young man named Bryan, who walked toward us from the reservoir's nearest edge. He was lanky, in his thirties, with exhausted, sunken eyes. He wore chest-high neoprene waders, a baseball cap, and a plain T-shirt, stretched and ragged at the neck.

"My dad's in there," Bryan said, pointing behind him, where houses sat in a lake halfway up their front doors. "He ain't leaving."

Bryan stood dripping in his waders. He lit a cigarette.

"He's an old stubborn son-of-a-bitch," he said. "A disabled vet. I called him this morning, asked him, 'You goin down with your ship, Cap'n?'"

Bryan's father had no flood insurance (it had only recently been offered for the area's homeowners, and at impossible rates), so his reasons for staying were a mix of the sentimental and the desperately financial. Bryan's father wanted to be there to save what he could, and if he couldn't save anything, he wanted to watch it all drown. He had a boat, which he'd tied to a tree in the backyard. He planned to hop in when it got bad, but not until the very last minute. Bryan seemed at once disapproving and reverential. I asked him where he would go while his dad watched the climbing waterline. Probably back to his own apartment, Bryan said, or the Marriott by the airport, where he worked. Or a bar.

We left Bryan there, smoking in the intersection. Nigel pointed us south, and we drove toward the Gulf, toward the Houston of my youth.

Water lapped at the underside of the vehicle as we passed through more residential districts. The Jeep could clear two feet easily, but on a few occasions, we looked in the mirror to watch the boat lift off its trailer and shimmy behind us, then ease back onto its carpeted runners. Suddenly, in an especially swift-moving stretch of current, while attempting to make a turn, we heard a sharp crack underneath our feet. We lurched forward, and the engine slowed to a limp. The whole chassis seemed to lift. We were drifting. The Jeep's four-wheel-drive linkage had broken on some piece of hidden debris, and now we were floating, if only slightly, toward the rushing mouth of a ditch. We both remained silent in the cabin as Nigel yanked the wheel in a desperate effort to gain traction. At the last second, the tires found concrete and skidded underneath us, squealing in the water. We whipped around and retraced our path, seeking another route.

JUST MINUTES later, on dry land, Nigel and I passed homes where floods had already come and gone, where people had started the process of mucking the unsalvageable remnants of their dwellings. I saw curbs buried in the waterlogged debris of every home. Families carried out their ruined belongings by the armful—the stacks of books and photo albums, the couches and recliners, the sagging rolls of carpet, the jagged and mounting planks of damp sheetrock, drapes, shoes, and mattresses. We traveled whole blocks where it smelled, as Nigel put it, "like the inside." All that saturated junk filled the air with the scents of indoor living—of potpourri and wet dust, ancient cigarette smoke, grease, and mold. The piles of garbage rose, each home's mound touching the next one as they spread, forming a continuous, steaming berm that traced the road. The city's trucks would come and haul the trash away eventually, but not soon enough. It would take months to shift and compact these domestic remains onto landfills around the state. As they waited, the mounds festered. They seethed, in the humid, post-storm heat, like giant and filthy altars to loss.

THE SETTLEMENT of Houston wouldn't have risen to prominence at all, most believe, had it not been for the toll of storms in surrounding towns, most notably the Galveston hurricane of 1900, which still haunts the streets and beaches of Texas's historic port town. On the afternoon of September 8, preempted by little warning, a howling cyclone arrived on Galveston's shores and took the entire coast by surprise, bringing with it a destructive mass of pressure and heat, unfathomable gusts of rain and wind, and a powerful wall of water. Without the aid of modern-day radar and meteorological warning systems, most residents were caught unaware, going about the natural course of their day. The hurricane's surge, which reached as high as fifteen feet, swallowed the city whole. Brick and stone buildings were flattened, and 3,600 homes were washed away. Cemeteries released the interred to the ocean's current, and bodies rose up, floating through the streets by the hundreds.

St. Mary's Orphanage, a campus that housed nearly a hundred children under the care of sisters from the Catholic Diocese of Galveston, endured one of the ordeal's worst tragedies. After retreating to one building's second story and binding children to their waists with lengths of clothesline, the sisters watched the surge dissolve the dunes and uproot the salt cedar trees that lined the beach. The water continued to rise and eventually overtook the orphanage. The building lifted off its foundation and disappeared into the swell. The roof collapsed. All ten sisters drowned, along with ninety-one of the orphans. Three children survived and were found clinging to a tree. Days later, the bodies of some sisters were discovered, their arms still clutched tightly around the waists of children.

After the storm, the smell of death clung to Galveston, and the problem of disposal forced residents to resort to mass burial. For the sake of efficiency and sanitation, the dead were loaded on barges by volunteers, weighted down with rocks, and dumped overboard. In the days and weeks afterward, some bodies loosened from their bindings and floated up, only to be collected again, bound into a floating mass, and burned in funeral pyres.

Galveston's 1900 storm killed nearly ten thousand and displaced an entire region. It prompted the once-thriving hub of Texan export to consider its fragility with new urgency. In the years following the disaster, the island began building a fortress against itself. Engineers designed a seventeen-foot seawall that could brace against future surges, effectively raising the town—every single building, street, sidewalk, and sewer pipe—to perch cautiously above the coast. The wall's first phase of construction took two years, and crews poured approximately one hundred feet of concrete a day while burying the structure's pilings. The structure itself required more than ten thousand railway carloads of granite, steel, sand, and wood, and the process of raising the town involved the painstaking use of massive jacks to suspend the place, sixteen blocks at a time, as they filled the new foundation from the bottom up. During the operation, Galveston's residents traversed the town on foot by way of an elaborate catwalk system, striding high above the disarticulated city. When completed, the seawall's sloped face formed an earthen border between the town and its people, a concave shield that traced the shore for three and a half miles.

Meanwhile, in Houston, the opportunity for new industry buoyed the city's residents. By the turn of the century, oil had been discovered in vast quantities throughout the state, spewing from the derricks planted in farmers' fields, marshes, and pockets of desert out west. Automobile manufacturing had reached a steady clip nationwide, and suddenly Texas found itself the country's bountiful supplier of petroleum. Augmented by the increasing cultivation of rice and cotton throughout Texas, Houston had the opportunity to position itself as the gate through which the region's most lucrative exports could pass. After a series of lobbying efforts put forth by local politicians, the construction of a colossal, deep-water port in Houston threatened to overthrow the hub of Galveston—previously the region's largest exporter—before the storm-weakened town could even regain its footing. Plans to deepen the creek-sized Buffalo Bayou and cut a fifty-two-mile-long, twenty-five-foot-deep path from the Gulf to Houston for the use of shipping barges were set in motion in 1912. The process involved two years of continuous dredging, including the addition of a spacious, half-mile-wide turning basin for the maneuvering of ocean-bound vessels near downtown. Portions of the bayou's shore that remained forested and overgrown with vines were razed, and construction crews scoured the bayou's banks to allow clean passage of ships. Houston at last entered the "deep-water era," linking itself to the intracoastal waterway and becoming—as the Allen brothers had ambitiously foretold nearly a century earlier—one of the busiest terminals of commerce in the South.

At the deep-water port's christening in September of 1914, President Woodrow Wilson fired a cannon at the site via remote control from his desk in Washington, D.C., and the mayor's daughter, Sue Campbell, stood above the dredged bayou to bless the project's completion. "I christen thee Port Houston," she announced, dropping a fistful of white flower petals (roses, not magnolia) into the murky water. "Hither the boats of all nations may come and receive hearty welcome."

———

THE STORY of this place has always been the story of war waged against water. Its buildings and the land that holds them are marked by the scars of past storms. Some recall their names with the reverent and painful memory of the dead, rolling them over like stones on a shore—*Carla, Katrina, Rita, Ike.* Most of the names are awkward, seemingly incongruous in their formality, laced with a delicacy that belies the savage deeds of the Gulf. They do not fit. Still, the host of titles persists. Each is an incantation built into the coast, carved by wind into the rotting and abandoned homes along the beach, their pilings bowed and splintered underneath.

Driving toward the Gulf, the effect of hurricanes on the natural world is brutally present. The handiwork of storms can be seen in the windswept dunes, their tops sculpted like delicate mounds of coiffed hair. The way every species of coast-dwelling plant—the big blue stem and plume grass, cattails, and sea oats, all of them swaying perches to countless tiny, vibrant, migratory birds in winter—roots itself at a permanent tilt. The way groves of squat oak trees grow on the beach, serpent-like, with limbs gnarled from decades of resistance to the shifting winds. The way sand and salt accumulate in every nook and crevice, the endless cycle of saturation and sun. The upturned boats that line the road, their hulls splintered and hollow, victims of a decades-old flood. There is a cautionary yet enduring way about the land. The environment carries a peculiar form of desolation, as beautiful in its hardiness as in its soft decay. This is the culture of storms, the generational toughness they breed. A storm contributes as much as it devours. Storms are the language through which this place communicates its loss, its survival.

My early memories are shot through with the cunning paths of rivers and storms. The constant presence of water— its wild capacity, the mysterious will of its movement—was a regular companion, a patient teacher and friend. I learned to brace against the regular disturbance of floods, accustomed to the low-grade hysteria accompanied by each forecast of heavy rain. Chores of preparation followed the news of each depression brewing far off the coast: The hammering up of plywood on every window, the hoisting of beds and furniture onto bricks and upturned buckets. The ominous rumble of clouds. The hot winds, sideways rain, and rotten-looking, greenish hue the sky assumed.

Most alarms ended in stints of harmless boredom—a day of canceled school, stranded at home, watching the rain accumulate. In their houses, each family watched as water lapped the curb, then the sidewalk, then up the subtle slope of the lawn. Overcome by boredom, the neighborhood's restless children often escaped their homes and joined friends in the rain. There, we devised games in the new landscape made by the storms. Wading up to our knees in the streets, we made boats from magnolia leaves and notebook paper, filled them with our make-believe passengers, twigs and acorns, then released the vessels and watched them drift, gradually sinking, toward the nearest rain-swollen storm drain. With bicycles and rope, we pulled each other through the flooded culverts, surfing on inflated inner tubes and blocks of Styrofoam. In lost and idle moments, feeling anxious or unsure, I have felt myself drawn to the water in subconscious and unexpected ways, as if magnetized by relation.

In 2005, when the angry brunt of Hurricane Katrina reached the coast of Louisiana and Mississippi, leaving millions without shelter, Houston welcomed the mass of refugees who migrated there. Displaced families came by the thousands, many of them with nothing but the clothes they wore upon rescue. They slept in our stadiums and spare bedrooms, enrolled in our schools, found new jobs and homes in Texas; many stayed. My high-school classes doubled in size that year, and the hallways grew packed with the new faces of the storm's teen refugees. I made new friends, developed new crushes and rivalries. The transfers assimilated quickly enough. They tried out for my high school's sports teams, and they played under the ironic flag of our mascot—the Hurricanes—tracing the groomed turf in their cleats during football games on homecoming night.

The storm made a lasting impact on the South's fauna, too. For years, local animal shelters remained packed with dogs rescued from the flooding in New Orleans, and my own family took in foster pets that summer, including two gangly cats, an elegant Boxer, and a rambunctious Labrador we named Samuel.

The following summer, working my first job as a janitor for an animal shelter not far from school, I wandered the kennels at night with a broom and mop, reading the biographical placards that accompanied each animal. Most still had collars and appeared relatively well cared-for, but when left alone, they howled the intense, rumbling howls of the abandoned. Late in the evening, after the veterinarians and their assistants had clocked out, I communed with the strays. Abandoning my assigned duties, still dressed in my issued scrubs and nametag, I'd open a cage, leash a dog or two, and break them free of the quiet building. I'd take them on long walks, winding through the dark streets of their new home.

THE CALM following Katrina was short-lived. Just a month after the storm, with the images of a drowned New Orleans still heavy in our minds, we watched another hurricane, Rita, enter the Gulf and aim itself directly at Houston. The storm's strength and trajectory sent the coast into a frenzy. Motivated by the extent of destruction and human loss in southern Louisiana, the city urged the public to evacuate en masse, as soon as possible. Most Houston residents heeded the directive, taking to the streets in a synchronized migration. But the plan backfired, resulting in a city-wide traffic jam on every west-bound lane. Drivers sat for hours, even days, on the congested highways. Many ran out of gas and water, abandoning their vehicles to hike or hitch rides back home. As a heat wave swept over the city in advance of the storm, the throng of evacuees sat sweltering in their cars. More than a hundred died from heatstroke while they waited, sweating and dehydrated, for the line of vehicles to move.

Meanwhile, my own family—either suspicious or ignorant of the advice to leave—decided to stay. We bought provisions: cans of chili and fruit, batteries for the flashlights, and extra kibble for the dogs. We filled jugs with tap water in the kitchen. As the skies darkened and the air chilled, I spent a day handing armloads of blue plastic tarps up to my stepfather, who perched on a ladder and stapled their edges to our window frames in preparation for hellish wind and whipped-up debris. Once we were finished, tarps covered every inch of the home's glass, and the place went dark.

When the time came, though, Rita failed to live up to her threat. The cyclone weakened upon landfall. The storm had spared us, for the most part, but for a few days we remained holed up, sheltering in place among the web of tornadoes spawned by the hurricane's unraveling coil. Throughout the night, the wind snapped the tarps angrily against the windows. Occasional flashes of lightning filtered through our new shades, and for those moments we lived in a magical, glowing womb of tarp-blue, as if dunked in an aquarium.

———

THE ABUNDANT motif of water bred unlikely salvation. Once, as an impressionable and grace-seeking preteen, convinced of eternal shame for my sins, I approached a kidney-shaped suburban pool and curled my toes over the ledge of its cement bowl. The time had come, I'd decided, for divine commitment. I stepped into the pool's shallow center, and there I joined a robed man—my childhood church's pastor— who grasped my nose with one hand, cradled my skull with the other, and plunged me into the chlorinated stench of baptism. Beneath the surface, for multiple disorienting seconds, I heard the warped sounds of scripture recited from above. I heard the resounding chant of "amen," the eerie ticks and creaks of the pool's drain, and the rushing *clomp* of water thumping against my ear. Then I felt a hard pressure hit my spine, and an uplifting force took over. My eyelids clenched, and the pastor brought my body back into the light of the world.

This was the year I learned the innate danger of the brain. This was the year my mother, who had been diagnosed with bipolar disorder when I was an infant, suffered her worst bout with the illness and was admitted to a hospital, isolated and stripped of contact. The symptoms had drifted in, ghost-like, and taken hold. In the tightest grip of the sickness, she spent days under a fog of sadness, lying prone on the couch, immovable and in tears, paralyzed by an unseen dread. Her rhythms were a riddle I ached to solve, and we became strangers to each other. Thoughts of suicide and fantasies of escape had driven my mother from me, and my own dark imaginings as her son—that I was to blame, that I had triggered or repelled her in some way, that I was not enough to prop her up, and on and on—began to creep in. I became tender and volatile toward the world, a teenager quick to thrust angst and judgment at anything that moved. Eventually, through a delicate cocktail of drugs and treatment, she learned to cope, but when she returned there were wounds in our relationship that had yet to heal. She was my mother, still, but a distant seed of distrust had been planted.

Thereafter, we were a family vulnerable to rapture. We were a unit hungry for release and affirmation, and that was the year we all grasped, accordingly, for the shining promise of the gospel, swooped up by the golden abstraction of the Word. We fled to the church, taking refuge in ritual.

That summer we baptized more souls of eager youths, and some born-again adults, gathering around the makeshift setting of our services. Due to limited funds and its fledging status, our church was nomadic, a congregation adrift. We had no legal home, and instead roved among repurposed venues: gymnasiums, hotel conference rooms, and vacant barns or garages owned by congregants. When we performed them, the baptisms took place in any available piece of water large enough to hold a body—from horse troughs to kiddie pools, and even, once, in a shallow slough of the Brazos River, where our pastor stood in his white robe, caked from the waist down in mud.

Each Sunday morning was a new adventure into the city and its surroundings, a new exercise of the imagination. Church events felt more like an act of fantastic theater than a moment of biblical dedication. The worship services, energized by lively music and impassioned sermons, led us into a sensation of collective euphoria, a pleasant distraction from our sinful, material lives. In the church, we could escape the boring cages of our bodies. In every crescendo we stomped our feet, closed our eyes, and raised our hands to the heavens. We felt the sweat build underneath our formal clothes, and the room grew hot with the intensified breath of believers. After the service, beaming but exhausted from the work of praising Jesus, my family would drive to Luby's, a ubiquitous cafeteria chain in Houston. We'd mound our trays with helpings of fried chicken and macaroni and cheese, tall cups of sweet tea, and bowls of chocolate pudding. Working our way through the cavernous dining hall, winding past other post-church families, we'd claim a table and feed, desperate for calories, like a band of devout athletes.

When my turn came to be baptized, I surrendered completely. I accepted the role as a turn of better fate, a chance at a new and enlightened start. That morning, I donned my swimsuit, memorized my scripture, and reported to the service, anxious and inspired. After the deed was done, when I arose from the pool and the congregation applauded, they greeted me with a beach towel. I rejoined them, shivering and saved, on the plastic lounge chairs scattered across the pool's deck. I was, again—though I felt no different at all, had experienced no internal transformation, as I'd hoped—born into the wet reality of this place.

4

ARCHITECTURE OF FAITH

NIGEL AND I continued to work our way outward from downtown. Winding through one neighborhood of ruined houses, we stopped when we spotted someone waving us down from the side of a residential street. He was an elderly Pakistani man, tall and trim, still dressed in his striped pajamas. His large glasses were askew on his face, and what little hair he had was piled high, nest-like, on his sweating head. He looked as if he'd just slept for days or else not at all. He'd been waiting all morning, he told us, for a chainsaw crew that had said they were on their way, and he appeared embarrassed when we told him it was not us, that we were not the crew, that we had no saw. After helping the man toss a roll of carpet on his own pile of debris outside, we were invited inside for tea. Nigel stayed outside, sprawled underneath the Jeep, inspecting the broken transfer case, and the man led me into his house. In there I saw the familiar mark of the flood: the bare concrete, the smears of mud, and the naked studs where sheetrock had been ripped away to allow the home's guts to dry. I followed him deeper inside, where the man's bed sat under a mountain of drywall and insulation. The night before, he told me, he and his wife had awakened to a crash and the loud tearing of drywall, then a strange weight on their sheets. It was the ceiling. A tree had punctured the roof, the joists had snapped, and rain had poured through a jagged hole.

Back outside, I summoned Nigel to the backyard and the three of us braced our shoulders under the tree's trunk, attempting to free it from the house. It budged slightly, then settled back into its cradle on the broken roof with a wet thud. The man would have to keep waiting for larger machinery and more help before there was any chance at protecting his house from more rain. There was no way to know how long that would be.

JUST BLOCKS away, in the yard where she'd finished tossing the waterlogged boards of her kitchen cabinets, a woman told me how she'd filled the bed of her truck with a thousand pounds of rocks to keep it from being swiped by the strange currents of the flood. When the water came on, cresting its tailgate, the truck stayed pinned to the driveway. She watched the flood isolate her home, rushing underneath the cinder blocks that held the place up.

"I know how to roll with a flood," she said. Her name was Sabrina, and she wore a faded T-shirt from Tulane University, which she'd fashioned into a crop top. She'd moved to Houston just a decade earlier, from New Orleans, where she'd watched the flood spawned by Katrina rise up the walls of her bedroom. Of all the curses and disruptions Harvey had brought, Sabrina was most captivated by its unexpected gift of free and convenient disposal.

"We just hung our butts off the porch," Sabrina told me, with no prompting whatsoever, detailing how she'd relieved herself in the days spent wishing the water down. "Just hung our butts off and went," she said again, "and let the water take it."

You could throw anything off the porch, she told me— shit, toilet paper, ramen packages, empty bottles, sodden linens—and the water would simply, dutifully, *take it*. What the water didn't take was left soaked and unusable, sunk into the thick mud.

The whole city had sunk, too. The weight of all that rain, resting heavily on the city's thin crust—an earthen layer hollowed out from underneath by the past century's extraction of oil, gas, and salt—had pushed the city down by a full two inches in spots. Where the rain hadn't gathered, people were stuck watching it rise from shrinking islands. They waited in the elevated quadrants of the city and sought out minor hills near their homes. They toted choice belongings in the awkward, makeshift luggage of black trash bags, and they crossed ditches and culverts on the tops of inflatable mattresses. They stood on roofs. They called, from their phones, and from the hand-scrawled signs of cardboard and wood, all manner of requests for rescue. When unreachable by boat or truck, and lucky enough to be spotted from above, evacuees cowered under the pounding *whump whump* of an approaching helicopter. They reached out to ropes, climbing inside baskets lowered precariously down to them in the rain.

EACH FACT and figure of the storm's toll hit with a surreal blow, and after making my way through the city with Nigel, talking to people cut off by the flood, entering their homes and hearing their stories, I'd begun to assemble a list of the ways in which a storm could level the lives in its path. It was more than flattened houses and life-or-death. More than ruined photo albums and the swamped engines of cars. It represented the particular strain of anxiety that had permeated the city, put on by the subtle but crushing phenomenon that so many had experienced in some way or another, in their bedrooms or on the street, within an instant: that there was water here—a lake, a rushing river, a shore—where there had been none before. The litany of accounts formed into a collective explanation of how that condition might play with the mind, how it might send one into a bizarre, extended haze of panic.

THE CITY rests on a buried fortune of decay. Giant, subterranean salt deposits tell us this area was recently an ocean's floor. As geologic faults shifted and brushed against one another to the west, forming mountains and dry highlands, the coastal plain remained underwater until it rose, at last, on a bed of salt, sediment, and a form of sand-like particulate called *chert*.

Under this thin sponge of mud and chert, layers of salt

formation lie staggered along the eastern portion of the state, forming massive columns beneath the city's surface, the tops of which bloomed long ago, slowly, with immense, patient force, pushing up pockets of oil and sulfur as they ascended. These flowering bulbs of salt hurled themselves upward, breaking through rock and clay. From deep underground, floating through more dense materials of soil and rock, they moved like the shimmering, elastic bubbles of a lava lamp. Most stopped just short of sunlight, where they hardened into shape. In some cases, the crowns of their bald, white heads emerged, noticeable as ever-so-slight undulations on the earth's surface. On the edges of these domes, wedged in basins between aquifers and bedrock, oil collected in deep pools.

You could eat the salt that sits under the Texas coast, but very little of it reaches our tables. The raw material underneath the city faces a series of varied fates, harvested and sold in rock form, transformed through a complicated chain of processing at home and abroad. Acquired by a host of interested third parties, the salt is ground, packaged, and used for highway deicing, or mixed with water, turned into brine, and repurposed in the production of industrial and consumer goods, from pharmaceuticals, to chlorine and caustic soda for swimming pools, to the PVC pipes that line a home's walls.

In the process of extracting oil and salt from underneath Texas, the earth around the salt domes held its shape, leaving behind large caverns. These caverns create valuable square footage underground, which is sold, or rented out by the companies that emptied them, as storage space. They become lockers holding fluid—oil, mostly—or injected with natural gas, waiting to be piped, or shipped, or driven in trucks to its final destination.

These husks remain, stoic and deep, nestling their sacred pockets of oil, marking time. The explosive bubbles hang in the bedrock like deadly balloons, and the makeshift bombs of their contents still haunt us. The giant underground salt fields from which they originated indicate the recession of an ancient, inland beach. They are a kind of ghost shore, a history so far removed from ours that it is challenging to accept. This place's perpetual fate to flood and drain is the burden of all that live here—knowing that their homes can return, quicker than they were built, to an original, Texan sea.

IN EARLY searches for oil in the Texas plains, drillers relied on crude speculation. Prospectors prayed, crossed themselves, and recited chants. They followed the trembling tips of witching sticks, divining the ore, puncturing the ground on superstition and blind faith alone. The early method, cable-tool drilling, sent a weighted drill bit into the earth over and over, raised and dropped by a thick rope, each time chipping away at soil and rock. Sometimes the bit hit clay, sometimes it hit stone, and other times it hit giant, underground oceans of salt.

The first major strike in Houston came in 1906, in Pierce Junction, south of the city, and the geyser set off an influx of profiteers. Houston was the next big gig. Investors and surveyors—*wildcatters*, they were called—came from all over the country. They bought giant tracts of land from farmers, then sectioned them out and sold them, bit by tiny bit, for exorbitant prices, along with the inflated promise of riches.

Across the ocean, amid another continent's race for oil, a geophysicist named Conrad Schlumberger sought to improve the unsophisticated methods of mining. He believed in a science of the trade that could transcend faith and superstition, one that could distill the act into a practical science. Conrad tested his method in France, in a bathtub in an apartment in Paris. He filled the tub with sand and rocks, planting coins at staggered depths. He lowered a wire into the sand, then sent a series of electric pulses through the tub. The nature of those pulses revealed slight variations in the content they passed through, and by examining the data, Conrad could map the mock ground of the tub. He could pinpoint the coins.

After testing the technology to scale on their estate in Normandy, Conrad and his brother, Marcel, set out to survey a swath of land on the coast of Romania. Conrad knew that if he could discern the contents of his apartment's tub, locating those pockets of tiny metal, he could find oil the same way. In Romania, near the Black Sea, Conrad and Marcel sent electrodes into oil-bearing salt domes not unlike the ones found up and down the Texas coast. They created a surveying company under their namesake, Schlumberger Limited, which would go on to become the world's largest and most advanced oil services corporation. The procedure they pioneered became known as "well-logging," and the Schlumberger Array was the technology that brought it into practice.

In the 1930s, keen on the recent drilling developments in the area, the Schlumberger company established its North American headquarters in Houston. The area quickly began to expand to develop the infrastructure needed to support the new Schlumberger operations. Not long after, Conrad's son-in-law, John de Menil, who was married to Conrad's daughter, Dominique, took over management of continental jobs. By then, oil deposits in every hemisphere had been tapped by the Schlumberger Array.

John and Dominique de Menil lived in Houston, and they became prominent socialites. They were French, both with degrees from the Sorbonne, and they spent their money—the mounting bundles of it—on an enormous collection of modern art. Their tastes were eclectic, and their collection favored artists whose work reflected life on the fringe. The Menils sought out and purchased so-called "outsider" art from prisoners, hermits, and self-taught artists, many of whom led unassuming, blue-collar lives while creating large bodies of abstract work: unknown collagists, folk painters, surrealists, aboriginal craftspeople, and the like.

When they'd married, Dominique, raised a Protestant, had converted to John's Catholicism, and the couple soon subscribed to the teachings of Marie-Alain Couturier, a French priest who pioneered the *art sacré* movement. Couturier's philosophy sought to fuse the spiritual with the artistic. It dipped into ecumenism, shirking ritualistic deities for more personal and abstract forms of awe. *Art sacré* wrenched the dull aspects of religious art into the realm of the contemporary art object. Dominique became friends with popular artists of the era, among them Mark Rothko, Jackson Pollock, and other abstract expressionists of their ilk. She believed in a kind of worshipped brand of art, bound to the ritual of religion but free of denomination, and she believed in its necessity in Houston, where she'd settled after leaving

France during the Second World War. She mounted a campaign for sanctuary-making, building an intimate museum in the city, now known as the Menil Collection, a subtle but profound expression of her wealth and spirituality. She knew even more than her father did that the act of mining was not above the miraculous. It was not immune from the holy, the aspiration that we might send tools and bodies down with a prayer and a charge.

As an extension of her philosophy, in 1971 Dominique built an open-faith, meditative art sanctuary on the grounds of the museum, the Rothko Chapel. It was a stark brick structure filled with fourteen massive paintings she'd commissioned, all of them dark, wall-length oceans of black and red. The building was open to all, free of charge, and became a fixture in the center of the city, a quiet home of reflection among the growing noise of capitalism and construction. The chapel stood in harsh contrast to the legacy her father had built. It was a drastic effort to still the manic vibration that had invaded the city in the past decades of the oil boom. In the face of quickening technology and rapid extraction, the brutish monuments to petroleum, Dominique's chapel represented a gentler, yet revolutionary turn *inward*. Inside the chapel, stepping in from the rain and heat, surrounded by the enormous canvases, visitors engaged in a refreshing, irreverent sense of design born from the city, an all-encompassing architecture of faith.

———

PUNCTUATED BY storms, a steady current of art and spirituality runs deep through Houston's history. Using the Menil art campus as their nucleus, several outsider artists (creators who were otherwise rejected or dismissed by the conventional art world, through various means of discrimination) had shot tendrils of creativity out onto the coast over the years, and much of their work had been displaced by storms or lost to obscurity.

In the moments before Harvey hit, I'd been thinking about Houston, the Gulf Coast, my roots there, and an abstract artist named Forrest Bess. A queer artist and fisherman born in 1911 who hardly ever left the Gulf Coast, Bess was a self-taught painter whose bold brushstrokes echoed his dreams, the land around him, and his experience of sexuality in the coastal South. By the middle of the twentieth century he'd amassed an impressive catalog of canvases and writings, but his life and work underwent a traumatic turn when his home was destroyed by Hurricane Carla in 1961. Carla made landfall in Matagorda Bay, in nearly the exact spot where Harvey first slammed into the coast and began its descent on Houston. Bess lost much of his work in that storm's surge, and it ruined him. He suffered bouts of depression that worsened in the solitude of his remote shack on the coast, and after Carla swept through he spiraled deeper into mental illness. His portion of the coast was wounded, economically and spiritually, beyond any timely repair. After discovering his work in a small museum exhibit in Chicago, I became fascinated by Bess's relationship with the land of the coast, as well as the rough history of extraction and industry that paradoxically kept the region afloat.

The physicality of Bess's pieces demands attention. His brushstrokes move like gashes, and the paint seems extracted from some dark, alien ore. He claimed to have worked codes into the patterns, allusions to theories he found essential to his work's appreciation, held by custom frames—ones he'd carved himself, from chunks of driftwood found near his camp. There was a wild grain to his work, clear spots where he had scooped sand from the beach and smeared it into the paint itself in an attempt to embed himself and his place, quite physically, into the canvas.

In an early block print made during a visit to Mexico, Bess toyed with abstraction, the blended grid of roof tiles in Taxco forming a crimson sea underneath him. In one work titled *Oil Field*, he resurrected the landscape of his youth, the rigs his father worked among towering over a splotched, indecipherable plain. He'd grown up in a mosaic of oil towns. His father, Butch, had shuffled the family to camps that sprang up, boomed, and quickly died around successful wells. As a child, every time Bess looked up at the horizon, instead of the sky, he saw the harsh lattice of drills. He was born into the oil boom's most turbulent period, when the new knowledge of oil had the whole coast trembling under the weight of descending prospectors, their machines, and the anxiety of fortune underground. Bess's was a family *on the move*, and his earlier artistic efforts felt like strategies to quiet that motion, to pin it down in stark, primary colors.

Bess's paintings illustrate a timeline of increasing strangeness and experimentation, beginning with simple landscapes and morphing into a projection of the internal world he struggled to understand. In the paintings he made after the Second World War—and, especially, after Carla—Bess's style moves into denser, more associative territory. It takes turns that can't cleanly be traced.

Bess's art existed alongside the abstracts of his era, but his work took on a kind of feral nature others didn't. He wasn't as much outside the abstract tradition as he was *uninterested* in it, in service to a separate muse: the land, and his position on it. Bess's work emerged from that place. It was born of it. I was attracted by that impression, that imprint. Dominique de Menil was, too, it seemed, and she served as one of his first notable patrons, purchasing his work to hang alongside more notable names in the quiet rooms of her gallery. In a way, Bess's paintings felt like the home I'd been scratching toward—irreverent and murky, delicate at times, touched by water and wind, permeated by the legacy of drastic profit and poverty.

Houston, the city itself, its image and memory, was an unexpected incubator for those kinds of wild ironies that Bess's work held in the balance. I wanted to name them. Over the course of multiple years, I'd made trips out onto the Gulf and into the city before the flood, on boats and on foot, trying to understand what made that culture possible.

FOR MOST of his adult life, Forrest Bess lived in Chinquapin, an unincorporated fishing village near Matagorda Bay, situated between Houston and Corpus Christi. He'd built his own house from the scraps of boats, a place that looked as if it would set sail when storms hit. The hull of an old tugboat comprised its walls, and the roof was made up of sheets of copper torn from the deck of a retired ferry. On the home's eastern half, Bess fashioned a concrete prow that pointed seaward, as if the place had run aground in reverse and settled, docked on the sand. His own paintings hung on the walls.

The driftwood frames were rough, pocked with holes from corroded nails. They lacked the delicacy of mitered corners.

Bess came from a family of coastal Texans, and his mother, Minta, an artist of sorts, suffered spells of depression. The family said there was "bad blood" on her side, and they wondered if Forrest had it, too. In his letters he composed lyrical odes to the Gulf:

"I have been thinking of the love of beauty," he wrote to Betty Parsons, his art dealer in New York. "All my life I have been an outsider looking at beauty . . . What I have here is a canvas and I am living in it."

Bess's intuitive sense of the Gulf somehow facilitated the visions he incorporated into his work. Its hardness spoke to him in a language he could translate.

In the mornings, he'd set out in his trawler, dredging shrimp in the shallow flats. He'd light his pipe and admire the birds, the sun, or the empty gloss of the bay's surface. On the side of his boat hung a sign, *BAIT*, and he sold shrimp to fishermen on their way out for the day.

"The peninsula is a lonely, desolate place," Bess wrote, "yet it has a ghostly feeling about it—spooky—unreal—but there is something about it that attracts me to it—even though I am afraid of it."

WORKING MY way through Bess's papers in the Menil archives, I began to read his ekphrastic portraits of the land he wrote in the letters to other artists and friends. He held a unique respect for the place. He loved its weather, the work, the fishing:

. . . a feeling of good companionship—then off to one side the trout school to feed and above them the gulls fly and circle and soon the skiff is in the middle of it all, and then it is a case of cast-cast-cast, a fish each cast and you are tense as hell, good god, we're short on bait, hurry hurry hurry and then it's all over, trout gone, birds gone, bait gone, nerves relax, time to smoke, and as you pull anchor and crank the motor you notice the wind is up, the bay is choppy, you head for home and feel the good clean salt spray in your face, you laugh at your friend when his ass leaves the seat and you can see daylight under him with each wave and trough . . .

In September 1961, Hurricane Carla made her way toward Bess and the coast, collecting winds and heat across the Gulf. She churned, a dancing coil of pressure and static, gathering thermals like a skirt. She twirled north, hooked west, and slammed into Bess's patch of land with more force than any recorded storm since. Winds reached 145 miles per hour at landfall. The brunt of Carla's surge sent a wall of water inland. Docks ripped from their pilings. Boats capsized or drifted for miles along flooded roads.

Carla was the first hurricane to be tracked and broadcast on live television using the National Weather Service's new radar system. On television, in the city, evacuees watched the hazy blob of her pulsate underneath a transparent scale map of Texas. The sight was unnerving but effective. People left their homes, Carla hit, and the coastal islands drowned under her surge. The storm spawned more than two dozen tornadoes, which skittered north on their own jagged courses through Oklahoma, Missouri, Iowa, Wisconsin, and farther still. Back in Chinquapin, Bess's home and at least eighty others disappeared.

"He's been sleeping in the remains of an abandoned shack," one of Bess's friends from Houston wrote to Betty Parsons after a visit. "It's the strangest, saddest story I've ever seen or heard. Kind of like as if Socrates had walked the ruins of the Agora, trying to find something of what had been."

FORREST BESS identified the same contradictions within himself that exist in the landscape of the Texas Coast. "There are, in my makeup," he said, "two distinct personalities. Number one is the military engineer, the oilfield [sic] roughneck, the accomplisher of missions well done. Number two is weak as a jellyfish. He suffers much, thinks deeply, and is quite passive in nature. Number one was reality, the oil fields, mud tents, struggle. The other: the child who hid in the sandbanks, and spent the day watching clouds and gathering flowers." He wrote to Parsons once, in a rare moment of displacement, from a residency in Woodstock, New York: "I feel like a pelican in a church."

He sent Parsons regular updates from the coast, reports on the conditions of his mind, the fishing, his work. At night he dreamed in wild symbols, and in the day he worked them into his paintings. He'd try to find their resonances in the early records of Aborigines, in Jung, in Goethe, in Herodotus. His pictures were meditations he thought possessed the power to impact viewers, physically. "I can make them hear music and then stupidly fart" he wrote, referring to his work *The Origin in Tone and Noise*. "I can make them yawn and then actually see sheep" (*The Symbol of Sheep*).

A gay man in rural Texas, Bess struggled against the persistent lack of acceptance of his sexuality. There were the occasional covert visits from fisherman, disguised as bait transactions. But the romantic possibilities of Chinquapin remained sparse and oppressive. Despite the outward freedom he possessed as a self-supported artist and fisherman, he felt like an artist hiding in his own skin, unable to communicate his true identity except through a kind of coded form of painting only he could decipher.

He became obsessed with studying and writing about the "hermaphroditic rituals" of indigenous cultures and was convinced he needed to re-create them on his own body in order to fulfill a path toward eternal life—his fountain of youth. He distributed copies of his "thesis" to anyone who would read it—an expansive, hybrid, and at times indecipherable document championing the restorative, transcendental effects of hermaphroditic alteration, a series of incisions Bess sought to have performed in his groin to facilitate penetration and heightened stimulation. He saw traces of this practice in the early alchemists, in the ancient Egyptians, in the child psychology of Bruno Bettelheim, and in the self-emasculation of Attis in Phrygian and Greek mythology. He wrote letters to Carl Jung, sent him regular notes on improvements to his thesis. When Jung finally wrote back, the great psychologist said, "What you have found is not unique. It has been found possibly once a century from the beginning of time. It invariably leaves the individual with the feeling that he has made The Great Discovery."

Bess was discouraged by Jung's response, but his convictions didn't change. During the first surgery, which Bess performed himself, he got "good and drunk." He doubled over himself in his shack with the tools, then passed out. He'd made a hesitant but deep incision near his scrotum. He was lucky the blood clotted.

The year before Hurricane Carla, he wrote to Parsons, elated. He'd found a surgeon to perform a second, more complete operation. "This makes your boy Bess a pseudo-hermaphrodite," he wrote. "The surgeon had no idea of the thesis, but he did it because he wanted to make a trip to Acapulco."

———

UNTIL HER death in 1997, Dominique de Menil continued to accumulate a collection fit for her pioneering museum. She and John hosted frequent salons in their Houston home where artists like René Magritte and Andy Warhol were regular guests. Their inventory grew with surprising diversity, sprouting unlikely juxtapositions, placing ancient Mesopotamian figurines and Mayan urns alongside the modern watercolors of Suzan Frecon and color photographs of William Eggleston. The collection's identity took shape beyond the bounds of traditional museums. The Menils were not siloed by a classic theme or a donor's expectations, but rather by their unique blend of spirituality and art. The only guiding principle, it seemed, was awe.

Dominique saw the frescoes first in 1983, in the twilight of her crusade for off-brand ecumenism. She bought the Byzantine pieces under suspicious circumstances, in a "dark apartment" in Munich. She knew they were stolen, but not from where. She believed in the spirituality of space, the idea that a traveler in the fourteenth century (or now, if she could fabricate the conditions) might enter the chapel near Lysi, a small Cyprus village, tired maybe, or doubtful, and look up to see a deity rendered. The space would be small, a closet of a church, enough room for the viewer to think but not to wander, the stone walls high. Around the original structure, under the bare stone dome from which Turkish smugglers had ripped the frescoes long ago, a grove of olive trees swayed. In Texas, there would be oaks. She designated a plot of land where the pieces would be displayed, adjacent to the Rothko Chapel. The oaks were planted, and a small foundation was poured. Dominique matched the interior curves to the brittle fragments of the frescoes, then mounted the shards so they glowed in the noon sun.

DURING THE week I'd spent searching for glimpses of Forrest Bess on the coast in 2015, I had stayed at the home of a fishing guide, Clint, and his wife, Jessamy. They were in their sixties, members of the region's unofficial cadre of "Winter Texans"—the groups of retirees and empty-nesters who flee to the coast during the drab months from their homes in the Midwest or farther inland Texas. They come in RVs, swaying along the interstates or parked, their wheels chocked, electric cords snaking from the doors, in formations dotted up and down the Gulf. Some come for vacations and decide, like Clint and Jessamy did, to stay.

Clint and Jessamy lived in a bungalow on stilts in Port O'Connor, where they rented out a room. Before moving there, Clint had run a used-car lot in South Texas, and Jessamy had taught middle-school science. They worked hard until they retired and dumped their savings into a permanent getaway. Jessamy liked to walk the beach, take pleasure cruises with Clint, and stand on the balcony of their house watching the sun dip below the horizon. Clint liked to drink.

I drove through their neighborhood, a little lost, until I saw Clint waving me down from the driveway. He was barefoot, drinking a flute of champagne. In the house, he handed me a glass and filled it until the bubbles spilled over my knuckles.

"You're gonna need a steak," he said, after we finished the champagne. Clint had the grill going, and I was welcome to throw something on. Inside, on a muted flat-screen in a corner of the house, the Longhorns battled the Sooners. There was a lot of wood paneling, some overstuffed recliners, and one of those mounted electronic bass that sings, moving its robotic jaw to "Take Me to the River," when you press a button under its rubber belly. Clint let me test it out. He gave me more champagne.

It was the off season for guides, and he and Jessamy seemed bored. During the summer, lawyers and engineers from the city would speed down and pay Clint to land stringers of redfish and speckled trout from the deck of his skiff. Now, the winter dragged on. Bait shops closed. Biker bars boarded up their patios. The town hibernated.

Clint directed me to the only grocery store, a gas station really, where I wandered the aisles, picking up and putting down the fishing accessories, the spools of line, the bags of frozen bait shrimp, before I eventually selected a questionable rib eye, its color gone, the sell-by date unreadable. When I brought it back, Clint seemed pleased. He removed its tight plastic casing, dusted it with some rust-colored powder, and threw it on the grill next to his own grayed slab of meat. He'd graduated from the champagne to a plastic jug of scotch, filling a coffee mug with ice. Jessamy emerged from downstairs with three collapsible TV dinner tray tables, which she unfolded and planted in the living room.

While the steaks seared, Clint dug into a drawer and pulled out a rolled map of the coast. I'd told him about Forrest Bess, and the occasion for my coming here. I'd told him about the house made of ships. In recent history, fans of Bess had tried, with the help of a few hand-drawn maps on his letters, to locate the exact coordinates of his hermitage. But what had they wanted to find, and what were they likely to find, exactly? A slab of concrete, maybe, or a pile of nets.

"Here's where your artist was," Clint said. He traced a contour line with his thumb. It was a bare patch of coast.

Clint and Jessamy and I watched football and ate the steaks in our respective recliners, hovered over our respective trays, and before I finished eating, Clint had knocked clean out. He'd drained four mugs of the scotch.

"He's had a long week," said Jessamy, and retrieved his plate, scraping the remnants into the trash.

I watched Clint snore, his head thrown back, his body limp and posed, altar-like, underneath the animatronic bass. There were other animals mounted on the wall, bucks and pheasants Clint had hunted in seasons past. They formed a border near the ceiling, their coats and feathers brushed flat, their skin shellacked, their eyes plugged with lifelike spheres of glistening epoxy. Jessamy came back in the living room.

"There's something you've got to see," she said, trailing off, and returned with a binder of newspaper clippings held in plastic sheaths.

Jessamy's clips narrated a local feud over a rash of accidents in town. Cars were colliding with an unprecedented number of large mammals on the road. People were getting hurt. The culprit, some said, was the unlawful introduction of a new deer species. Some wealthy rancher had taken to hunting exotics on his property nearby, and he'd been raising these imported beasts shipped in from the Himalayan foothills. They roamed a low-fenced parcel by the man's house and escaped sometimes, reproducing, and appearing dangerously on the roads at night, big as elk, dumb to the threat of traffic.

"Just popping out of the fog like that," said Jessamy. "Crazy." She flipped through the glossed pages, guiding them gently over the binder's rings. "These wild creatures from India or wherever, right under our noses."

The next day, I asked Clint if he'd take me on his boat out to the island that butted against Bess's suspected hermitage. Matagorda was one of those slender lengths of land that marked the intracoastal waterway's perimeter, about twelve miles long and two across, uninhabited except for a few seasonal state park employees. My plan was to visit the place and take stock, to walk any ground that I could. I wanted to see what was left, a generation past its abandonment.

In the early 1900s, the island sustained a few successful cattle operations. The Hawes family settled there in the late eighteenth century, finding the island harsh and secluded, but financially tenable, safe compared to the rollicking, fly-by-night sugar boom that was under way on the nearby Brazos.

Still, the logistics of island cattle-grazing proved an uncertain enterprise. The Haweses moved their cattle on crude rafts across the bay. They weaned the cows onto the tough and fibrous grass that grew on Matagorda. The gamble worked, and the operation thrived, isolated and exposed as it was. The Hawes family made a living. They made a home, first in canvas tents, then in a clapboard house that rose on the island's northwest shore. They raised families there. The kids grew up catching and releasing jellyfish in wooden buckets, listening to cranes squawk overhead, and watching movies projected onto strung-up bedsheets at night. All the while, the primary and inescapable dread, of course, was the seasonal battering of storms.

One night the Hawes house flooded during a tropical storm's surge, and the family retreated to a high dune with their blankets and jewelry, the water chasing after them. They fell asleep as the sea rose, and hours later, when they woke, they found themselves covered in rattlesnakes, their bodies entwined, clinging to the last patch of dried earth. Pacified by shared doom, the snakes stayed limp as parents loosened infants from their grasp.

During the Second World War, the military seized the island and used it for target practice. The Hawes family was given ten days to pack up and move back to the mainland, taking their cattle and sheep along with them. They had no choice. They relocated, and over time the descendants dispersed. While the war dragged on, pilots-in-training strafed the land. They pummeled every inch with bombs, and on weekends took hunting trips on the island. Wearing thick boots and gaiters for the rattlesnakes that still coiled under bushes, they stalked the whitetail deer and coyotes that had survived their attacks.

On our way to the island, Clint and I wove among sandbars and grass flats on his skiff. He pointed out some notable sites, his favorite fishing spots, an old lighthouse in ruins. He stood at the wheel of the boat, getting sacked with wind and spray, while I cowered, frigid and shaking a little, in the protective nook of the bow. When we arrived, Clint helped me off the boat and onto a decrepit loading dock. He'd be back the next day around noon, tides permitting. I rolled out my nylon tent and settled in, sending stakes into the sand with a chunk of driftwood.

Before the sun went down, I took a hike through the vacant and strange desert of the island. I found the crumbling remains of the runway that had supported those training planes. The concrete was broken through, spiderwebbed with weeds and saplings. The rest of the island was filled with shallow pools of rainwater, all of them perfect circles, craters formed from the projectiles that had exploded there in the 1940s. A few drab, military housing structures still remained, buckled under their slumped roofs. Nothing else stood to stop the wind as it lashed across the island and howled in my ears. I felt, more than ever, absolutely alone, wandering, in search of no spot in particular but sure of the place's elusive importance. That whole island seemed to hum. It felt like the junction that was Forrest Bess and the crude project of Texan industry. It felt like an eerie center of all that history and longing. I reached the far beach and confronted the unobstructed expanse of the Gulf. It was bare except for a thread of fine trash and weeds deposited by high tide. A line of canine tracks dotted the sand, and I followed them as they skirted the dunes.

I wondered if Bess might have heard the explosions of

those pilots dropping practice bombs. I thought of him painting in his odd shack, or out on the bay netting shrimp, while the planes rehearsed their plans of attack.

Or, I remembered, he may have been absent altogether. Bess had served his own stint in the war, fittingly, in the Army's Camouflage Design Unit, where he and other artists plied their trade for the country, cutting plywood silhouettes of tanks and bombers meant to fool enemy scouts on the battlefield. The props they made were gigantic set designs in a live theater of war. A convenient disguise among disguises. The design unit was a kind of haven for Bess in the service, but it didn't last long. "I was an oddity and I didn't fit in," he wrote, describing the time he'd been badly beaten for coming out:

> [I] left Bay City and moved to Houston, and there I found protection in numbers with people I thought were my own kind—but I was too "butch," rough for them— war came—made an excellent officer—but I messed up once—too much drink and too much excitement— caved-in skull; lead pipe and facing court-martial and disgrace—requested transfer to San Antonio and art—I am a peculiar type of homosexual—there, it's written!

The coyote tracks disappeared in a tract of softer sand, and I abandoned the pursuit. I went back to the tent. I thought, before going to sleep, about the host of eccentricities packed into this place, about Bess's birds and fish on the bay, about the wild instincts of the cranes. I thought about Jessamy's strange animal mysteries, and I dreamed of those giant sambar deer, lurking in the ditches and waiting on the turns of dark roads.

In the morning I woke to find the tent filled with thousands of feathers. A squad of duck hunters had arrived overnight, and they'd already returned with their kill. They were going at the breast meat with thin steel blades on the beach, tossing the carcasses. The wind persisted, and through some faulty late-night zippering I'd allowed the plucked down to whip through the vestibule and into my space, so that my home now resembled the insides of a ripped pillow, a snow globe of feathers. Duck down had slipped under my clothes and caught in the hinges of my glasses, and it fluttered through the tent, catching light.

5

FREEWAY CITY

I N A FREEWAY CITY, the collective imagination spans twelve lanes. Beyond their utilitarian role, our highways intersect a network of strange and random culture, a collective form of entertainment that plays out, perpetually, in dramatic and deadly terms.

I remember the chases most of all. As a child, at least once a month, I rushed to the television to sprawl belly-down on the carpet, propped on my elbows, hooked, while police cruisers raced through the local news, pursuing a car across the wide breadth of the highways. The scenes were tracked by helicopter, in shaky-framed, frenzied shots. The police cars had their sights set on a driver whose crime we rarely knew. Perhaps there had been no infraction at all, or, we speculated, perhaps the driver was a murderer, a violent criminal at large. Connected by the communal circuit of television, the city watched these scenes unfold, watched the fugitive pass familiar blocks and landmarks, or, on rare occasions, speed past the windows of our own homes. These are the spectacles that bind and shape us. These are the democratic measures by which the city understands itself, through the universal cinema of the road.

———

PERHAPS MORE than any other city, Houston earned its roads. Mile by mile, engineers struggled to tame the mud that blanketed Houston. They tried digging past it at first, carving trenches for wagons and livestock, but the rain persisted and formed sweeping, stinking bogs. The mud—*gumbo*, some call it—halted wheeled travel and annoyed pedestrians. City laborers stacked railroad ties, massive lengths of stone, and loads of sand and gravel, all of which sank or warped into useless ruts.

Like that of many other early coastal towns, the city's first bona fide road lay on a dampening bed of pulverized oyster shells. The shells, dredged from nearby bays and repurposed after their meat had been consumed, reflected sunlight from their mirrored insides, and the road shone like a gleaming strip of silver. When developers poured cement for the roads, they laid it thick as a runway on account of the shifting mud underneath—twelve inches in spots. You could land an airliner on that road, they said, and coast it to the beach.

———

NOW THE freeways, labyrinthine and fortress-like, occupy our horizon. Overpasses—the first of which must have seemed absurd to drivers, perilous even—dominate our vision.

————

I LEARNED to regard my home in this way, on the move, cruising on overpasses nearly two hundred feet high in my mother's rattling yellow Oldsmobile. I sat perched in the small cockpit of a child's car seat, the air-conditioning off, my calves dangling against the rough polyester upholstery. I watched, glued to the scene outside, as we ascended and descended, feeling the free thrill of takeoffs and landings. I remember the garish, pleading billboards whipping by, the exhilarating smears of neon, and the endless motion that comprised the rhythms of our daily commutes.

————

NOT LONG ago, an intrepid magazine journalist toured the city, taking time to observe its built and natural environment, navigating its roads and waterways, noting the peculiar methods of its residential blocks. He remarked, with some distaste and superiority, the way homes sat adjacent to industrial parks and refineries, chemical plants, and scrap yards. He was trying, it seemed, to nail down the particular identity of his subject. He was attempting, and failing, to translate the city for his reader, to discover its central *aboutness* and distill that into a neat, readable package. Eventually, skipping the normal pleasantries of description, he offered one blunt and dismissive summary: "Houston has a bayou: it smells."

————

As an entity, Houston is a city that struggles, at every turn, to contain and define itself. The city grows haphazardly, spreading and demolishing without nostalgia, rebuilding without the typical obstacles of residential building codes. It is the product of booms staggered throughout the last century. It is the only city of its kind, a bright and capitalistic assemblage, sporadic and irregular, largely unzoned and dominated by the whims of commerce, and it is a city formed in direct service to the freeway commuter. Laced and stitched with suspended interstates, Houston was built after widespread accessibility to the affordable, efficient car, built after air-conditioning and the tract house. It was a city designed to accommodate those who bought cheap land in the sticks, built a cheap house, and *journeyed* to work on smooth, wide-laned thoroughfares. The bayous wind underneath those roads, and the city's industry followed the queues of those roads and bayous rather than the patterns of foot traffic. Houston does not—the saying goes, spoken either as a point of pride or complaint—want you to walk.

Whole stretches of Houston's streets became driveable shopping centers, public spaces one could browse by vehicle, moving through aesthetic shifts in one drag, taking in the juxtaposition of necessities: A mile of washers and dryers, lined along the curb, in front of their brilliantly painted vendors. A sprawling region of Pick-A-Part junkyards, sprinkled throughout with restaurants and homes, followed by a school, then a cemetery, then a warehouse filled with water heaters, then an untouched quadrant of swamp, alive with egrets and alligators, then a tri-story strip mall of shops, salons, and mechanics, and a tower of billboards, their advertisements in any language but English. Beginning in the 1970s, the city established itself as an industrial hub and major exporter of goods. Vastly diverse immigrant communities came seeking opportunity, traveling from Vietnam and Ethiopia, Pakistan and Laos. They were drawn by the promise of affordable living, economic prospects, and a climate that mimicked that of their homelands. Once they made it here they planted roots, encouraged more families to come, and founded communities that stretched for miles throughout the accepting frontier of the city. Contrary to the experience of immigrants in other cities, when these new residents built businesses and homes in Houston they were not saddled with traditional municipal zoning laws meant to "standardize" construction and, ultimately, direct a type of growth endemic to a mostly white, affluent vision of America. Instead, the city's endless space and lack of regulatory laws made for a more welcoming if indiscriminate canvas. For the first time, as Houston expanded and flourished, its perimeter assumed the accessible, unimpeded ideal of the public forum, a gallery unbound by blocks, walls, or admission fees.

When the city first grew, it blossomed into a constellation of neighborhoods. Those neighborhoods emerged around refineries and rigs, around quickly built industrial centers, colonies of office buildings, warehouses, and airports. In Houston, "commuter subdivisions" were not an exception or afterthought, but the pulsing heart of urban life. The city formed itself in random and fascinating patterns, such that one could appreciate them, if they hadn't been conditioned to think otherwise, as uniquely beautiful. Taken in from above, or on an aimless drive down a thoroughfare, the city could resemble a surprising and contemporary installation of industrial art.

In their efforts to contextualize the city with urban theory, Houston's critics despised its unchecked model of development. They called it a "donut hole city," under the hypothesis that outward growth creates residential "rings" of affluence, which in turn cut off and strangle the communities within them until the city has no center, but rather a series of ever-widening, cancerous orbits of residence. The critics are taught to hate this model because they learned from cities like New York, and London, and Paris, and other European models of cities whose success, social and economic, relies on the thriving heart of downtowns, on the density of an urban nucleus.

But the critics were wrong about Houston. They refused to look at the pockets of community in the circles themselves. They refused—because it was easy to, and because it is always difficult, or unpopular, to name new culture as it bubbles up, unexpected and strange. In their refusal they glossed over an identity that was uniquely American, a product of all the borrowing and overlapping and scrappiness that identity entails. They looked at the way people had made their homes and businesses work in the suburbs, the wild and efficient mess of that scene, and they said, in so many words, ignorantly, *who cares?*

———

ONCE, IN 1993, an incident on the freeway sent the city into a period of collective grief. Late at night, a man named Jeff Alm, a professional football player for the local NFL team, the Oilers, took to the streets in his Cadillac convertible. His childhood friend, Sean Lynch, was in the passenger seat. The Cadillac's windows were rolled down, and Jeff was leaning his foot hard into the accelerator. He was climbing high along the incline of an arching overpass. The two men were celebrating a personal reunion, and both had been drinking, and as the vehicle gained altitude the air grew thinner and cooler. The city twinkled underneath. The riders, these two boys, reveled in the breeze, charged by the harmless bite of a Texan December whipping hard against their naked ears. Their adrenaline spiked. The highway was vacant, the sky dark and clear, and the vehicle's engine roared as they scaled that suspended thread of road into the bright night.

And suddenly the car jerked.

Something had gone wrong. Either Jeff had mishandled the curve, or the vehicle's tires had slid on the road's fine skin of oil and dew, or both men had abandoned their station altogether, dozing off. The car smacked hard against the guardrail. Jeff wrenched the wheel in an overcorrection, and Sean—whose seatbelt hung beside him, coiled neatly into the housing of its retracting mechanism—flew from his seat, clearing the road's shoulder and plummeting, his body limp and helpless, onto the surface of a road nearly thirty feet below.

Precise details of the event are limited to the sparse police report that followed, but after exiting the car, Jeff did a strange thing. Disoriented with whiplash, after leaving the car and observing the lifeless body of his friend below, he returned to the crash site. From a deep compartment in his vehicle, he pulled a weapon, a shotgun with a sawed-off barrel and pistol grip, and pointed it to the sky. Inexplicably, he fired three shots into the air. Then he crumpled onto the concrete. He placed his back against the retaining wall, then put the barrel to his mouth.

The city's residents speculated. In the fearful and ignorant way that humans do, walls of gossip and shame surrounded the tragedy. The tales, crude and sensational, reported all manner of fabrications—that Jeff was unsatisfied with his performance on the field, pushed toward death as an aversion to mortal embarrassment; that the men were lovers, repressed and ashamed, driven to death; that they'd faked their deaths and escaped.

We know only the bare facts of the matter. We know only the unexciting truth of forensics. We know the image of that Cadillac and its mangled front end on the highway, its hazard lights winking in the early morning darkness. We know the exact grade of the road, the temperature and humidity, and the unique cocktail of substances present in the two victims' bloodstreams at the time of death. We know the exact size of Jeff's cowboy boots, one of which was placed, peculiarly, as if thrown off, a short distance from where his body was found.

We know that the built environments of a place, by nature of their permanence and monstrosity, gradually work themselves into fables, and those fables, in turn, weave themselves into the fabric of a city's truth. We do not and cannot ever know the thoughts of those men, but I imagine, sometimes, when I am driving late at night, the fleeting sensation Jeff might have felt while standing on that highway alone. I imagine him there, at a loss for understanding, his friend dead and unreachable, the city a wild carpet of lights stretching out beneath him.

A FEW years ago, a woman gave birth on the highway. She labored in a van's passenger seat, stuck in traffic, while the father drove. They filmed the whole thing, and the video made its rounds on the internet. The mother's water breaks as buildings flash through the van's window. She lets out a fierce groan, straining in her seat, and just seconds later the newborn emerges, healthy and shrieking.

Stunned, the mother cradles her baby, slumped over the floorboard. The child—a ten-pound boy—is beautiful and large, coughing and sobbing, still tethered by the living rope of his umbilical cord. "He's breathing," the father says, shocked at the weight of new life. Then he switches lanes.

———

AMONG HOUSTON's proudest exports is the underground strain of hip-hop known as chopped-and-screwed, a creation of the iconic Texan deejay Robert Davis Jr. He, too, was a child of the road, and his body of work comes closest to a definitive art of the highway.

Davis came up from Smithville, Baptist country, pecan country, land of wholesome, starch-shirted, hardworking, come-on-inside people. Davis was a young boy of nine then, his father a long-haul trucker, his mother a house cleaner. He liked his mother's records, B. B. King and Johnnie Taylor, and he liked to drag them harshly under the player's needle, liked to make them skip and slag, sound inhuman, sound fucked up. Davis did not like school and quit. In 1984, he liked the movie *Breakin'*, liked Ice-T, liked Easy-E, liked to play *Galaga* for hours. He had a way, they say, with the joystick. When he did not like a record, he would scrape a drywall screw across its grooves, his cousin Trey saying, "Who the fuck you think you are, DJ *Screw*?" He liked that, too. Made that his title. When he moved to the city, he liked the feel of the land there. Liked its tangle of highways, liked the cars, liked the girls, liked the people in those cars that trolled slowly down Westheimer, their spokes, their slow jams, the thick air, the smoke, the Styrofoam cups of codeine and Sprite. Liked to fill mountains of gray Maxell cassette tapes with tracks he'd slowed down and cut up, scratched up, pieced together, recorded over—strange, syrupy music of some altered, unearthly people, out there, swerving their large-bodied sedans on those towering overpasses, their trunks unlatched and booming.

A collection of archival boxes at the University of Houston's library bears his name, each packed with ephemera. There are photos of Screw as a boy, in his Little League uniform, and photos of him posed, altar-like, kneeling before his mixer at home. There is a photo of Screw in his coffin wearing his blue FUBU jersey. There is a dry cleaner's coat hanger WE ❤ OUR CUSTOMERS owned by Screw, covered in erratic notes, names and lyrics pressed into the fragile paper between wiring—plans for an album, plans for samples and reworkings so urgent Davis reached for what he could and wrote with what he could. Some lyrics are written with glo gel pens in black-paged notebooks, some on business cards, gas bill envelopes, some on record store receipts, the margins of chrome rim advertisements, and some on wholly intact three-by-five Mead pads in precise, punching couplets:

Times are gettin' crazy
Feds they wanna raid me

Mother fuck the fame
I'm stay the same

He wrote the poetry of a town, watched it pass by in the window of his own car. I was four when they found those two football players, Jeff and Sean, dead on the highway, strewn out from the steaming mess of that Cadillac, and I was eleven when Screw was found, in a home not far from my own, unconscious from a codeine overdose. By then, Davis had filled every boom box and cassette deck in town with the pulsing beat of the city, the avant-garde map of his mind. He'd sold each of those tapes from his trunk, from his drive-way, in parking lots, from a grocery bag in the dark corners of clubs. People mourned his death nationwide, played his mixes on repeat and never stopped. We wore shirts to school airbrushed with his name, the entrepreneurial pioneer of our city's sound.

Every once in a while, art comes erupting, geyser-like, from the places it shouldn't be, and we're left ankle-deep in the abundance of it. *Where was all this genius churning?* people asked. *From what reservoir? Under which crust?*

———

YEARS AGO, during an exploratory drive across the city, I made a stop at the long-revered institution of Key Maps, Inc., in search of the highways' offbeat history.

Within moments of arriving at the shop, Jen Marie, the owner, kept telling me *you can't map a place this big.* We were standing in her strip-mall retail space on W. Alabama, sur-rounded by endangered tools of navigation. Globes lined the shelves, frozen on their tilted axes. Lit up by the late-morning sun, their colorful spheres surrounded us. We were in their orbit, a small constellation of wayward, plastic planets.

Tubes of laminated wall maps leaned in clusters against the walls, others were unfurled and pinned up for scale. That's all they really sell these days, Jen told me, post-paper, post-map-and-compass. Novelty stuff. Now the maps are in people's phones, the directions ready-made. There's no more *work* in finding your way, she lamented, and so the company's resorted to peddling the decorative, the aesthetic fluff, the fodder for therapists' offices and middle-school classrooms. After all, Jen reminded me—in a tone that was abruptly tragic, as if sacrificing her livelihood on the spot—who actually *uses* a globe these days?

But I could hear that machine still chugging away in the back. I could hear the steel contraption pumping out its warm sheets of maps destined to be sliced into shape and laced into spiral bindings. Its faint cadence was the soundtrack of the store.

Jen revisited her mantra. She rephrased.

"You can't map a place this big," she said, thrusting her arms out, framing a wide bracket in the air, "on a map this *small*," then brought her arms back in, as if collapsing a tourist-bureau accordion-style map, à la *Streetwise Manhattan*.

"The technology's not compatible," she went on, "unless you do it like us," speaking of the method her father, Jim, devised in 1957, when one night he grew unsatisfied with the navigational aids for his young town of Houston, frustrated by attempts to distill this rambling, indefinable mess of residence, these hundreds of square miles of odd-angled streets and lots, sprawling dead-space, undeveloped swamp, gas stations, subdivisions, "office parks," and on and on. In that moment, Jim spread an image of the city across his apartment's carpet. He smoothed the image across his floor, then sectioned the land into smaller squares with a ruler and marker. He made a grid, then broke that grid into pages. For every street he assigned a tidy, corresponding code, and for every code a detailed, full-color page. This was the only way to contain the city, Jim knew. From there he developed an exhaustive legend by which travelers might pinpoint destinations on the fly. The resulting product, the Key Map, became a standard accessory of every taxicab, police cruiser, ambulance, pizza delivery driver, et cetera. It became Houston's own *London A to Z*.

I wanted to visit Jim's shop—the one Jen inherited upon her dad's death—because I remembered these maps. Tattered copies sat in the floorboard of my grandfather's clanking Ford sedan. They rested on the dashboard of my school bus. I remembered finding my way inside of them, flipping through their pages and mouthing the awkward titles of streets—*Fuqua. Westheimer. Silber. Studemont*—charmed by their abstract-colored panels, the numbers I could not discern but regarded as a thrilling, foreign code. They were cubist puzzles I studied on long drives, a promise of both the strange and the certain. In a home devoid of most books, Key Maps served as my own private library, the vast and democratic literature of the land.

Like the best artists, I learned, Jen's father plagiarized. He borrowed his style of mapping from the Canadian Mounties, who used it to survey vast swaths of northern wilderness. In times of disaster, when the forests burned, these maps gave contour to what lay underneath the smoke. Parachuting firefighters, armed with only modest tools and masks, jumped into smoke on the faith of those maps. They plotted their falls, calculated drift, and plunged onto what they hoped was solid earth. Jim saw a similar need in his and his neighbor's own mundane travels. He imagined what worked in one wilderness might work in another.

Jen takes field-tripping kids on tours of the operation. She walks them through the production room, lets them ogle the gear and backstock, but they struggle to grasp the concept. They hold no memory of paper maps. In the digital age, of course, the maps are oriented for us. You are always at the center of your own atlas, always your own journey's protagonist. You are the pulsing blue dot carving a line through space. The physical map, on the other hand, requires surrender, patience, perspective.

To initiate them, Jen plays a familiar game. *Get inside the map.* Lay it on the floor. Smooth it out. Find your street, and hop on. Now where are you going? "Then the light bulb turns on," she said. "Then they get it."

I WAS and still am a zealous map kid—forever seduced by the prospect of treasure and scavenger hunts, of secrets and stashed-away loot. Bottles washed ashore with precious missives tucked inside. The mysterious prompts for questing. That enticing, unreachable *X*. The electrifying idea of following another's flawed, looping route. Isn't a map, after all, an act of trust?

Before leaving Jen there, alone in her showroom, I picked out a utilitarian piece: a four-foot county map awash in purple, yellow, and orange. It's a collage of jagged districts and territories. At home, tacked above the desk, it takes prece-

dence over most art. In lost moments—looking to gain purchase, or clarity, or confidence in the face of my own feeble
strivings on the page—I stand near it.

———————

THE WRITER and historian D. J. Waldie, chronicler of the
first American suburbs, speaks of the peculiar ache of domestic inheritance in *Holy Land*, his elegy to the street grid that
became the tract-house subdivision of Lakewood, California.
His words work toward the truth of what it means to wres-
tle with the memory and significance of one's homeland. To
live anywhere in America is to invest in the sins of place and
property. Every neighborhood, town, city, and sidewalk has
its own vibrant and pasted-over vein of memory. "We all live
on land wounded by our living on it," wrote Waldie, "yet we
must be here or be nowhere and have nothing with which to
make our lives together."

To Waldie, there was more to the suburban grid than
sterile repetition, more than boredom. There was a familiar
code laid over the homes, a shared language, a righteous pattern. A geographical prayer. He grapples with the cost of that
legacy and looks for it in the soil, in the territorial history,
and in the quiet but heavy dramas of civic life. "How should
one act knowing that making a home requires this?" he asks.
"How should I regard my neighbors?"

———————

AFTER HOURS spent winding through Houston and helping
in any way we could, bouncing from roadblock to roadblock,

Nigel and I charted a course for the abstract edges of the flood. My mother was still stuck, texting me photos of the waterline growing closer to her kitchen window. I wanted to reach her if I could, and I feared that if I couldn't, if the roads between us remained under deep and treacherous currents, I would be simply taking up space in the city, contributing to its spectacle of distress.

As the rain beat on, we kept driving, occasionally hopping out to check the depth of water on the road, then creeping slowly through it, careful not to stir a wake and swamp the Jeep's intake. I wanted to reach the Brazos River, the landmark I knew well from childhood and could use as my own gauge for the storm's damage. When we came upon it, the watershed was unrecognizable. The river, typically winding and indirect in its path, had jumped its banks and made a wide beeline to the Gulf.

In a subdivision abutting the river, a frenzy of neighbors hustled in and out of their homes, some fleeing and others coming back to see what the waters had done. Residents stood in the comparatively shallow water on their lawns, weighing the options to swim or to stay. Wading into the flooded bowl of the neighborhood's center, assisting an elderly woman with a trash bag full of her belongings, I felt the water rise to my waist, then to my chest. It was cold, stained by the filth of the street.

While crossing a particularly treacherous stretch with a mild current, I helped one evacuating family fetch a raft that had escaped and floated across the street in a gust of wind. The water was deepest on the street's edges, and at one point, just before I felt the curb under my foot, I missed a step and sank helplessly into a storm drain. For a moment I bobbed, neck-deep, my leg darting pitifully in the mouth of that hole. I took a deep breath, prepared to go under, and right then I felt how easy it was to be deathly careless in this place. Entering a frantic state, snagged by a shoelace, I clung to a cheap inflatable made for swimming pools. But the drain had no suction. There was no place for that water to go, and I eventually righted myself, grateful and ashamed.

On the neighborhood's outskirts, I watched a team assemble a length of giant pipe, which they dragged with a tractor and affixed to a pump the size of a house. The pipe arched from one side of the levee to another, over which the crew intended to tap into the subdivision's flooded section and "throw the water" into the swollen Brazos. The spatial implications were beyond my comprehension. Combined with the barrage of municipal updates we heard on the radio— the dam release rates, the chemical plant decay stats, and of course the mounting inches, fifty-one at last count, of cursed rainfall, the whole thing felt colossal and nauseating.

Military cargo helicopters circled us constantly, and humongous, olive-drab high-water vehicles rolled around corners, sloshing gigantic wakes. The chaos of the scene was an eerie flashback. The last time I'd walked like this with Nigel—the two of us on either side of a ruined street—we'd been overseas. Back then we carried rifles instead of life jackets. Nigel was a machine-gunner, and I was his team leader. Nigel's frame was sturdy and fast under the weight of his gun and the clunky, plastic tubs of ammunition. Over the years we'd developed an effortless rapport, communicating wordlessly on patrols, reacting with quick precision in moments of chaos. We'd trained together in Hawaii, and we'd navigated the island's mountainous jungles on fabricated missions, firing blanks at role-playing combatants, digging fighting holes as cover for the imaginary threat of mortars. We'd trained in the Mojave, in the giant expanse of desert owned by the Marine Corps, leading assaults on bizarre, manufactured towns built to resemble whole blocks of Baghdad or Kandahar. We'd spent weeks living in tents, around Joshua Tree and Twentynine Palms, patrolling and conducting range exercises by day. At night, the stars shone bright over our unit's campsite, our tents staked in neat rows on the sand, and we'd stay up, telling jokes and cleaning the fine grit of the desert from our weapons. We'd share the cigarettes and candy bars smuggled in our packs. We'd share intimate secrets and fears, dreams for the future.

Months later, in Afghanistan, that training translated into a muscle memory of brotherhood. Out of necessity and fear, too tired to complain, we survived weekly firefights and explosions. We stared for endless hours into the pitch-black desert while on post at night, concealing the embers of our cigarettes behind cupped palms. We protected the tight-knit family that was our tiny patrol base in Helmand Province. As a duo, Nigel and I were always in sync. And we both hated it. We longed for the release of civilianhood. When our contracts ended, we'd bolted in our own directions. I went to school, started writing. Nigel went fishing.

THAT NIGHT, we made a stop at my grandmother's home in a southwest Houston subdivision, where my stepfather's family, all Cubans, loving and loud, had taken to calling the

house "Southern Ellis Island." Many of them had evacuated
their own homes and made it, just barely, to her elevated
porch. They were two nights deep into a Harvey-induced
slumber party. We ate loaded plates of *picadillo* and rice and
beans, drank *café con leche*, and watched the news.

The popular perception by then was that Houston was
suffering an apocalyptic siege of the heavens. The broadcasts
placed death on every corner, a spin I hesitated to confirm.
Watching the coverage, I feared the city was sliding into the
fate of a community under duress, portrayed in the over-
simplified roles of desperate victim and generous, descending savior. I worried about my place within the constraint
of those characters, and the way I had, maybe, in my own
attempts to reach my family and take stock of the place, done
more harm than good.

But in contrast with the theatrical narrative of Harvey's
impact on television, I could also observe the more nuanced
truth of the city. The rescues continued in Houston, with
waters still rising in Beaumont, but as I saw it, the tenor of
the city at large rang surprisingly resolute. Among the neighbors Nigel and I encountered, for instance, no one had been
without a sideways joke about their flood experience. On
driveways and in gas stations, we witnessed people eager to
talk to one another about their stake in the event. On one
block earlier that day, bumping along in the boat, we met
a group of residents who stood gathered around a blazing
fire pit, swapping stories while they awaited more vessels like
ours to take them, one by one, to a dry shelter elsewhere in
the city. In the chaos of the flood, faced with the easy route
of self-preservation, their first impulse was to turn to one
another, their own ad hoc community. They lent tools and

food. They checked on relatives and coworkers. In their own ingenious, respectable ways, people were dealing.

The next day, around noon, I joined a sizeable gathering in an empty lot near a convenience store, where several families surrounded a folding table sharing a meal, the adults drinking beer. One woman stood over a mound of sizzling pork chops. The group welcomed me, offered me a plate. A few of the table-sitters poked fun at my shoes, a pair of old-school Reeboks I'd christened just the day before, wading in the Brazos-adjacent neighborhood. I laughed, kidded back, and attempted to hula-hoop for some giggling grade-schoolers.

THE NEXT morning, with the roads now semi-passable, Nigel and I, at last, reached my mother's side of town. She'd made it out of the house and had begun volunteering at a pop-up animal shelter in the parking lot of a mall. I watched her dunk her manicured hands into a bucket of warm bleach, then scrub vomit and feces from the floors of countless animal crates. I walked a brindle mutt from Pasadena named Ruckus. He had soulful, chestnut eyes. I saw more piles of donated Purina and Iams than I'd seen in any retail setting. I saw, from the morning and into the night, more than a hundred volunteers, strangers as diverse as the city itself, sweating, giving their time under the welcomed but blazing Texas sun. The animals came from all over the city, packed into horse trailers and vans—strays and groomed domestics alike—and they left as quickly as they arrived. We loaded them in sedans and SUVs, where they rode to shelters around Central Texas and beyond.

At the only open restaurant we could find, I watched my

mother drain two frozen margaritas with impressive haste. She was beat, dehydrated, and a little drunk.

"I can't believe y'all made it here," she said between sips.

She wore a stained and frayed T-shirt with her hair thrown into a messy bun. She wore no makeup, but she looked beautiful and tough in the way she always had.

Later that evening, back at the house, she walked me through the damage to her property. She and my stepfather were lucky. The house had miraculously taken on no water, but my mother's car had been ruined in the flood. A scum line indicated that the floodwaters had reached halfway up the small hatchback Honda. A pool of reeking liquid sat in the vehicle's trunk and floorboards, and random clumps of debris littered the yard.

Meanwhile, up and down the street, in lower-lying houses that had not been so fortunate, my mother's neighbors did more work to clear their homes of the quickly molding interiors. During moments when the flood was highest, boat crews had axed and sawed their way through fences to make paths while crisscrossing the city, and that lumber, too, lay perched on the growing piles of garbage. On a home nearby, a family had affixed a giant, spray-painted plywood sign, reading "NO WAKE," to their roof, pleading with passing boats not to send waves through their front door and cause even more costly damage. Now the sign leaned against the curb, wet and warped, its necessity past as quickly as it had arisen.

Sitting on the mud-slicked back porch with her, watching the bayou's waterline recede, I felt my mother's combination of fatigue and relief.

"Every storm," she said, "they always say the same thing:

Leave. But where are we supposed to go?" She was looking far past the bayou now, into the perversely stunning sunset the storm had birthed, a violent watercolor of pink and orange smeared across the horizon.

For a moment, it saddened me that I wasn't an option she considered for refuge in this way. We shared an ironic and stubborn resistance to help from others, and I knew that, but I was upset that I had not yet graduated in her mind to someone she could, and should—because I craved it—count on in times of strife and uncertainty. Over the years, our relationship had grown into a tender but awkward bond, and it felt like we both held each other at arm's length in the way two people do when they recognize too much of themselves in each other, keeping a distance in fear of watching their own strain of neuroses unfold. We were both pained by internal worlds, in one way or another, but lacked the courage or time to address them as a duo. I'd picked at this thread before, needling her unfairly about my childhood and her mental illness, but the conversation usually devolved into a fight or ventured into memories still too raw to explore. This reunion, at least, had the neutralizing circumstance of real emergency, and I was oddly thankful for that. It provided a handy counterpoint for our love, allowing us to see each other freshly, without baggage for a change.

When it got dark we hugged, in a way we hadn't for years, holding each other's backs lightly. We went inside, and she helped me carry a stack of blankets upstairs, where we made a bed on the floor for Nigel and me.

That night I slept the dreamless, granite sleep of a sunstruck and rain-pruned traveler. I wanted to stay in Texas, to see the storm and its flood through to the end, but I also knew the reality of my life outside of it. Nigel and I would leave the next morning. We had professional obligations. I had classes to teach. Nigel had promised his girlfriend a week at the lake.

6

WE HOLD OUR BREATH

B Y NOON THE NEXT DAY, Nigel and I were on the road out of Houston. By sunset we'd crossed into Oklahoma. The route took us under a bridge and past a quick interchange, then through the gates of a toll booth. Nigel was at the wheel, and suddenly I felt him smack a hand hard on the dash.

"Fuck," he said.

We'd missed the exit, and had begun driving down the long, desolate stretch of turnpike that angled east, away from Tulsa and through the Cherokee reservation's rural expanse of hills. As we drove, concrete retaining walls rose up beside us, and the land beyond them was a dense, sprawling green, free of homes. When the sun sank, no flickers of porch lights or bonfires sprang up in its place. The road itself was brightly lit and uninterrupted. We could do nothing but follow its route. When could we turn off? Where would it end? *Not until Missouri*, the woman had said at the toll booth. *Not until an hour.*

It was a scam, Nigel said, his logic spiraling into a rant. The confusing signage was intentional, he claimed. The state wanted to get you stuck on a course, headed off to nowhere, make you drive and pay, drive and pay, until you end up in some tiny casino town, pissed and tired, finally able to retrace your tracks. Nigel began to fidget in his seat, and I sensed the impatience coming to a boil in him. It was this easy restlessness that set us apart, the kind that could make him hot and shaking with rage in an instant. He got in fights. He frequently began and spoiled relationships. Sometimes I feared that volatility, and sometimes I envied it.

Years earlier, on a plot of land outside Tulsa where Nigel hunted each season, I'd watched him kill a rabbit at full gallop with a .22, making no use of the rifle's sights but firing, it seemed, from the pure and unteachable accuracy of instinct. He'd field-dressed it faster than I could process, grasping the creature by its soft ears and sliding his grip downward in one swift, clean motion. The rabbit's warm guts had spilled from a neat incision made near its anus. "A little trick I know," Nigel had said. He was quick like that. Smart and violently efficient.

The past few days had marked a shift in the union between Nigel and me. We shared a dynamic that had, increasingly, in the domestic years after the military, started to cool. Nigel regularly made unfulfilled promises to visit me in Iowa. He made and abandoned elaborate plans for fishing trips we would take on the coastal tributaries in British Columbia. We talked on the phone sporadically, but there were long periods when we were ghosts to each other. I knew Nigel had been in jail more than once since we'd been discharged, but I didn't know what for. He wouldn't say. I worried about him, even when he insisted I shouldn't. Three years back, when I'd gotten married and asked him to be the best man, he'd promised to come, but in the weeks before the ceremony he'd stopped answering his phone. He never showed.

Despite his inconsistency, I felt inside me an unwavering ability to forgive him. We were the kind of friends who could revive our closeness in an instant. I loved Nigel, and sometimes that love was hard to sustain, but in the past week together I'd remembered what drew me to him. Nigel was a caretaker. I'd experienced it countless times on patrols together in Afghanistan, and in the dragging, idle hours of standing post in the Iraqi summer, but those memories had started to dull. Now, I could see it clearly again. It was our shared mission, the fact that I genuinely needed him, and he had come through. It was the clean obligation of a storm and a flood, and my mother.

When Nigel talked about his own mother, he included nothing beyond the clipped, unfeeling tone of fact. That she had committed suicide. That there had been drugs, and a moving car at night, and the memory of several rough men, their quick entrances and exits into and out of his hazy child-world. That Nigel himself had been young, not yet eleven, and had gone to live in Broken Arrow with his grandparents, who still had thick German accents and made pounds of deer jerky in the garage each season. That she had lain there, on the shoulder of the road, for an indistinct period of time. That the report had concluded no foul play.

That's where they found her, Nigel said, after a chunk of mutual silence in the Jeep. We'd been traveling for half an hour, still headed in the wrong direction down that bright scar of road. *Somewhere up there.* He lifted his arm from the wheel and pointed. He was pointing into the road's far vanishing point, toward the state line, into a region—a place in conversation and on the map—that he refused to touch.

Before we could reach it, Nigel slammed on the brakes and jerked the wheel of the Jeep, maneuvering quickly in fear of some approaching trooper or sheriff. He ramped us over the sloped median, its high grass hushing on the machinery underneath, the boat jostling on its trailer behind us as we turned around. For a moment the headlights darted wildly into the woods, dark as tar. Nigel had deflected, as he always did, and steered us into more comfortable terrain.

WITH OUR direction corrected, the night wore on. Nigel and I listened to music. The wind whipped hard through the Jeep's cabin, and we had the volume cranked. Houston was still draining behind us, and I felt a mounting sense of shame for leaving behind such a scene. I wanted to keep the city fresh in my mind.

I have in my possession, both cerebrally and in the bank of my phone, an ever-improving Houstonian playlist whose tracks I ran through. I played Henry Thomas's "Bull Doze Blues," a song I've long believed to be Houston's most apt anthem, despite the fact that Canned Heat copped its melody for "Going Up the Country" in 1968. I played Guy Clark, and some of Townes Van Zandt's cuts from the Old Quarter. I even played some Geto Boys, and Barbara Lynn, and, for kicks, as we blew past the box stores, Arcade Fire's "The Suburbs."

It wasn't until I turned to the radio that the rush of feeling came on. I heard a station queue up Kenny Rogers and Dolly Parton belting out their classic duet, "Islands in the Stream," a song I'd heard hundreds of times before but never really latched on to. I'd dismissed its silly and cloying back-and-forth and considered its primary metaphor—lovers stuck in a hard-fought relationship, both stranded and bound by the river of struggle that surrounds them—the clichéd territory of Nashville romance. But now, in the vulnerable fog of exhaustion and nostalgia, I *listened*. There was emotional density and nuance packed in there. "Islands in the Stream" is a song in which Kenny merely assists, nursing it like a trivial player does a football before a field goal attempt, balancing it on the turf with a gentle index finger while the kicker, Dolly, stutter-steps and knocks the thing into a galactic, spiritual abyss. Something in the unbridled wail of her entrance, the liquid imagery, the peak of soprano when she admits, confesses, the aching paradox of her heart: that she's all at once lonely, bitter, in the dark, and still in love. It's a song of distance, of connection over water and enmity, of stubbornness, of making it work even when it shouldn't. A song of *resilience*, that word I'd heard thrown around so frequently on the news—on television, on the radio, and in the papers—to the point that it had begun to lose its edge, until now. The song's protagonists grapple in the dark for each other, they find purchase and grab hold of what they can. It undid me. At the key change I started bawling.

I tried to keep it together for Nigel, but when we parted ways in Tulsa and I was alone in my rental, I found the song on my phone and listened to it on repeat. I let myself sink in the seat, set the cruise, and had a healthy, sustained cry until Kansas City. I thought about Houston and the coast behind me, the sunken streets of my youth, and I thought of Bryan's stubborn father, the man who waited alone in that wet room on the edge of Addicks Reservoir, his boat floating out back. I understood that illogical love of one's home. I'd also violated it. I'd left Houston, like a coward, like a lazy lover hopping islands. And then I'd come back and left again.

ONE OF the men who raised me, my stepfather, works as a policeman for the city. A Cuban immigrant, his family emigrated to Houston in the 1970s. Driven by an opposition to Castro and a desire to fulfill a sense of American opportunity, they boarded a plane with only what they could carry, entrusting their future in a young city across the Gulf of Mexico. When they arrived, seeking a community of like-minded and Spanish-speaking expats, the family settled in the neighborhood of Sharpstown, the city's first master-planned subdivision.

In 1955, Sharpstown became one of the nation's first neighborhoods designed to accommodate automobile-owning families, as well as the first to incorporate an extensive air-conditioned shopping mall. Frank Sharp, who planned the neighborhood, intended for the community to house the teams of astronauts training at NASA's new facility on Nassau Bay. Early marketing for the neighborhood bordered on the evangelical, and the language of the community's advertisements took on the mid-century hyperbole of spaceflight. The living rooms of Sharpstown homes would hold the families of the first lunar teams. The sports cars of astronauts would glide smoothly into their garages, and the neighborhood would shine with stainless steel and chrome, a glittering image of space-age luxury.

"You are invited to attend Houston's greatest home building event," read a 1955 advertisement in the *Houston Post*. Residents from surrounding communities—potential homebuyers Sharp wished to recruit—were encouraged to attend and view the plans set forth for the subdivision. The developers made a gesture of the event, filling a time capsule on March 13, 1955, with a curation of trinkets meant to be unearthed in the new millennium. Ultimately the astronauts did not move to Sharpstown, but my stepfather did, along with his brothers and sisters, and his parents, and his aunt, and his grandparents—all of them in one house on a block filled with other Cubans, each of those families in their own identical brick homes.

In the pockets of urban wilderness surrounding the neighborhood, my stepfather and the neighborhood's other kids explored their new settlement. They fished for bass and bluegill in the ditches, and they rode bikes and homemade pushcarts, *chivichanas*, through the freshly paved streets of Sharpstown. They dodged the occasional barrage of rocks thrown by surrounding, Texas-born kids, who thought their broken English strange and threatening. Packs of children gravitated toward the homes whose owners had splurged and fitted their backyards with the pale blue bowl of a pool. Those houses became a refuge in the city's permanent summer. In the blinding glare and unmistakable, chemical stench of those pools, they played, and re-created a facsimile of the homes they had left behind.

These days, on his way to work, my stepfather passes the streets where he grew up. He passes the bayou his home bordered, and the field where he played baseball with other kids who learned to throw curves and changeups in the streets of Havana. Every night, as he has for the past sixteen years, he feeds a revolving gang of feral cats on the corner of Beechnut and Bissonnet. He shouts *C'mere kitties*, and they emerge from beneath the dumpsters. He piles food on the concrete and waits, like my mother does with hers, for the cats to finish.

On the job, he patrols the bayous in a white sedan, and he confronts the minor frictions a metropolis churns out. Early in the mornings he finds drivers, drunk, passed out in empty intersections, their feet still on the brake pedal, their trucks idling while the lights change. With a surprising grace—one whose source I cannot begin to comprehend— he sneaks up, reaches through the window, and eases the shifter, without waking them, into park. Responding to 911 calls, he enters the homes of families in the throes of dysfunction, placing his body in between quick flashes of domestic violence. He carries out this task with the memory of a boy displaced, the boy who arrived so many years ago and could not speak the language.

One year, while driving past the banks of a bayou, he saw the foot of a woman rising from the water. At first he was unsure. At first he thought, *mannequin*, until he saw the sock, and then he wondered for the first time in his life if mannequins wore socks. He moved closer. The woman was pinned to a discarded shopping cart, drowned. The night before, she'd left the apartment where her family lay sleeping and walked toward the water. She'd taken some pills, walked across the street, passing the quiet homes of families at rest, then made her way gracefully down the steep embankment of the bayou. There, she stood before the gentle, shallow current. She removed her robe, folded it, and placed it neatly on the concrete shore. Then she stepped in.

—

BEFORE SHE met my stepfather, my mother had spent two years ferrying us and our things between short stints in various homes throughout Houston. We camped out in the apartments and small houses of unfamiliar men, in the spare rooms of relatives, on couches, on pallets made from quilts on the floor, and on flimsy, foldout mattresses. Each move was abrupt, frenzied, and marked by the ritual of packing our belongings hastily into the trunk of my mother's car, a large sedan, boxy and yellow, which she piloted across the city when each time came to uproot. Together we wove through the city with the windows cranked down, my mother at the helm, her hair tangled with wind, looking determined and wild.

—

IN THE wake of Harvey and other storms and their cycle of floods, there are widespread critiques of how the city's lack of regulation, particularly its rapid swapping of permeable earth for concrete, has made the area prone to severe, uncontrollable flooding. In the effort to manage the bayous as free-moving drainage systems, concerns have been raised about the hazards—and mysteries—of so many open bodies of water. The city knows the bayous are clogged with garbage. Reports claim the bottlenecks and bends of Buffalo Bayou, as well as its major tributaries—Simms and Braes—are obstructed with hundreds of abandoned vehicles. The vehicles could solve a stack of open homicide cases if recovered, but only if the city were willing to invest in extraction. In the wreckage, some say, are the forgotten and long-missed bodies of the dead. One citizen investigator saw the drowned cars on his sonar equipment in 2011, when he was searching for a missing elderly woman named Lillian High. He says he gets regular calls from families, asking if their own loved ones might be "under there." He told the city. He offered to help. They said it would be too expensive. The process would take too long. The divers would not be able to see through the muck.

Even before the flood in 2017, the city knew the watersheds would swell and crest their banks, and the tides would spill into homes and streets like they always have. They knew the bayous would seize at their gates and confluences, the debris would form dams, and the city would morph into a shallow and ever-broadening extension of the sea. No dredging or preventative extraction of trashed cars would change that. No political maneuvering or reform could outsmart it. No sandbags could hold it back. Faced with the reality of rising seas and increasingly fierce tropical storms, the city sits poised for a more vulnerable and disaster-prone future. The entire coast lives under the omnipresent threat of immersion. There is, as they say, nothing we can do. We hold our breath.

Still, under the weight of that reality, I watch my mother react with stubborn loyalty. I watch her adopt strategies against the erosion of this place and, at times, it seems, of herself. In her car, she roams the neighborhood's outskirts at dusk, a glass of Diet Coke in her lap, and she takes photos of abandoned, soon-to-be-demolished farmhouses. She slips under barbed-wire fences and rubs her hands along the engravings of headstones in overgrown, forgotten cemeteries. She sprinkles scraps of food along the perimeter of her house, soliciting her colony of fostered animals from the thinning woods. She reaches her arms around this place and embraces, pulls inward, erecting her own personal, disaster-proof ark. *You should not live here*, the continued reports and statistics seem to suggest, yet she keeps accumulating, keeps digging herself in. *We are sinking*, they say of the city, and she buries her heels deeper.

———

IN AN attempt to comment on Houston's urban abnormality, and its position as the only major city without a formal land-use policy, a conceptual artist came to the neighborhood of Sharpstown in 2010, bought a house, and did something that shocked her neighbors. She flipped the place around. With the help of a construction crew, several trucks, winches, and trailers, the artist, Mary Ellen Carroll, detached the home from its foundation, jacked it up, and rotated it, gradually, until the structure had turned exactly one hundred eighty degrees. Then she set the home down, refurbished its interior, and let it sit. She preserved the home as a public exhibition, unoccupied, embedded in the neighborhood.

Carroll chose Houston, and Sharpstown specifically, because it represented a convenient case study into how the city's lack of zoning directly impacts the lives of its residents. When the postwar subdivision of Sharpstown was introduced, it was the nation's largest community of single-family homes, and while it began as a subdivision marketed to the city's aspirational white residents, it quickly became, by nature of Houston's accessibility, a convenient and prosperous destination for immigrants from Cuba, Vietnam, India, and elsewhere. Later on, during the explosion of malls and chain stores across the country, the area was overtaken by retail. Parts of the neighborhood were demolished or encroached upon by businesses, and eventually Sharpstown dropped out of the city's admiring eye. Lots of people, my grandmother among them, stayed in the houses they'd been in for so long, but other homes were vacated, left to decay unnoticed.

By using Sharpstown as a vehicle, Carroll hoped her artistic gesture would prompt discussions around land use and the urban condition of the city among residents. She wanted to disrupt the idea that every space in Houston, residential or otherwise, was destined to be ruled by fluctuations of the market, by free enterprise, and thus, in many ways, be made inhumane, out of the individual citizen's control. Rotating the home was an attempt to resist the city's machine of growth, while simultaneously emphasizing its potential for eccentricity. In her own words, Carroll sought to "make architecture perform" through a ready-made art object—in this case, an abandoned house, its back door pointed toward the street—while at the same time "avoid[ing] the snare of the artist as displacer, gentrifier or developer."

One critic from the *New York Times*, Joyce Wadler, was not convinced. "If turning a house 180 degrees is art,"

Wadler asked, "what do you call a house being driven down a highway?"

"A house being driven down a highway," said Carroll.

The rotated Sharpstown home was still standing in 2017, but after Hurricane Harvey upended the lives of thirteen million people throughout the South, causing $125 billion in damage, much of it residential, Carroll reconsidered the exhibition's purpose. Exactly seven years after she'd picked the home up, she chose to destroy it. Dressed in a suit, cheered on by fans, filmed by reporters, and heckled by annoyed neighbors, on November 11 she drove up to the home in a yellow Caterpillar excavator, lowered the steel jaws onto the home's roof, and tore it down. It took less than two hours to flatten the building. The home's remains, Carroll said, would be interred, piled in a heap within the city limits as a memorial for victims of the storm. She named the pile "Mount Harvey."

As a child, early in the morning, when my stepfather returned from work on the night shift, I'd watch him perform his daily ritual of decompression. I'd watch him remove the heavy leather belt and Kevlar vest, watch him place his stinking boots near the door, and I'd hear the hard thud of his pistol on the dresser in the bedroom. Then he'd return to the kitchen, take a seat at the table next to me, and wrap his hands around a fizzing glass of Coke. With my mother still asleep, I'd sit and listen to his stories—long, intricately woven plots of his evening, accounts of violence and abuse too obscene for me to interpret. We sat there, in the dark quiet of so many mornings. "Last night I found a woman," he might begin, his voice trailing into the soft lull of a poet's.

My stepfather's stories were ones he could not help but tell, a compulsion I now recognize as a common reaction to trauma. In those stories, he built a harsh, spoken map of our home and its surroundings. He assigned feeling to each street name, each building, each curving body of dark, brackish water. And in turn, during times of emotional upheaval and angst, amid the violence and fracturing of our family, I dreamed of escape. Plagued by bad luck and trouble of my own making in high school, I backed myself into a corner of desperation. I felt trapped in my city, surrounded by dead ends and lacking purpose. Long after dark, I took solo drives on the vacant streets. At night, when the retailers closed and the strip malls went to sleep, the only light came from military recruiters' stations tucked between nail salons and smoke shops, their entrances cast in neon, the uniformed men lounging inside, waiting. At night, my part of the city was dead and silent, and I, in need of instruction, naïve and restless, vulnerable to myths of freedom and power, looked for a way out. I moved toward the lights, entered those bright chambers, and signed.

7

AFTER THE STORM

IN THE FALL OF 2018, long after the floodwaters receded
in Houston, I stood at the feet of one of Texas's most iconic
structures, waiting.

The event, we are told, will arrive as a violent geyser of
water, propelled from underground by brutal proportions of
electricity and pressure, then focused into a vertical torrent
and launched heavenward (two hundred feet above ground,
give or take) in a spectacle designed to mimic the discovery
that hurled us into the modern age of petroleum and made
Texas—for all contemporary intents and purposes—*Texas*.

Here in Beaumont, at the Spindletop–Gladys City
Boomtown Museum, about eighty miles east of Houston, a
small crowd has gathered to pay tribute to an oil well of chief
distinction. The affair's attendees—mostly parents and their
restless kids, tourists set free from the jostling chambers of
their vehicles—are hunkered a safe distance from the appa-

ratus, swaddled in coats and hoodies. It is cold for Texas, and frigid especially for Beaumont, which is almost as far south as the Gulf shore, nearly nudges southwestern Louisiana, and lies along the roaring, six-lane path of the country's southernmost interstate highway, I-10. When our preliminary tour of the premises ends, the museum's director, Troy Gray, a meticulous, gentle man in synthetic hiking pants and a tucked-in charcoal sweater, steps into the courtyard and makes the call. In exactly five minutes, the contraption will blow. "You might get wet," he warns.

Prior to the announcement, Troy led his audience through a replica town built alongside the well complete with a drugstore, livery stables, a printing shop, and an active blacksmith studio enclosing an intimate "town square." The excursion crafts a detailed illusion of the region's most turbulent age—the early twentieth century—when the whole state erupted in an instant frenzy of new industry. His speech is hurried yet precise. Troy takes pride in the ambition of historical accuracy in every scene. He smirks, blushing a little, singling out the curated details of chamber pots and brass spittoons. In the barbershop, ducking under a protective velvet rope, he pauses to note the room's period chairs and marble sinks, the hand-painted signs offering FULL SHAVES and HAIR SINGES. There's a boarding house, too, and a funeral parlor and a spacious saloon with a functional wooden balcony from which, Troy claims, once a year, to the amusement of local children visiting on a field trip, the museum hires actors to toss an ornery drunk into the street—a stuntman, miming a brawl.

And of course, in a wide field beside the museum, rising high over the surrounding neighborhood, visible from the highway, stands the facsimile of the derrick itself—the imposing, sixty-five-foot structure, a symbol designed to inspire in us some brief and amplified awe of the past, an appreciation for the ingenuity and courage that brought us here, the wonders of science and superstition so tightly wound into the history of wells. The spell works.

Not long after Harvey's first anniversary, this region still limps from the blow of disaster. The wounds of that year persist, from the visible toll on infrastructure to the unseen yet palpable strain among people. In a tangle of complicated ways, both Harvey-induced and not, my attendance at the Spindletop museum marks an emotional homecoming.

During the lasting aftermath of the storm I'd realized, somewhat ashamedly, that my motivations to go to Houston during the storm had been tainted by fatalism and greed. They were seeded by those initial childhood impulses to observe and record the failures of my home, to sketch them out in my own privileged narratives. Similarly, my trip to Spindletop serves to stoke that childlike fire of interest, recalling the same person that scoured the woods around defunct plantations as a kid, hunting for clues in the disappearing fragments of lives lost to wicked empire.

Who among us has not seen the image of the erupting oil well or at least composed it in their imagination? Who is not seduced by such theatrical displays of fortune? That absurd black fountain of crude bursting forth, roughnecks dwarfed by the derrick, their faces freckled with treasure. The fodder immortalized in *Giant*, *There Will Be Blood*, and *The Beverly Hillbillies*. The cartoonish fluctuations of wealth and despair, luck and hope, played out in a visceral stream of black gold.

Successfully tapped in 1901, the original rig wouldn't have been constructed had it not been for the near-biblical resolve of one man, a Beaumont entrepreneur and reformed hooligan named Pattillo Higgins. Born in 1863, Higgins, also known as the Prophet of Spindletop, believed from a young age in what lay underneath the sulfurous hill outside his hometown, professedly assured by a divine voice. He spent fruitless years hatching failed plans, drilling shallow, unsuccessful wells, perforating the land to no avail. He struggled for funding. Neighbors and friends called him foolish. Reporters claimed he was a delusional crank who knew nothing of geology and had only "witched the hill with a peach limb," as one journalist, Robert Shackleton, wrote in the *Saturday Evening Post* in 1901. Many times, he nearly gave up, urged on only by the buoying force of his premonition. As he aged and the hill sat dry, his chorus of detractors multiplied. By the turn of the century, the gift of vindication loomed.

In the winter of 1901, a crew of workers toiled over the mouth of a stubborn well. Up to this point, no human had managed to harness deposits of petroleum with any notable scale or efficiency. Oil, in its scarcity, remained a novelty substance with unrealized potential, used primarily for lubricators, solvents, and kerosene, found floating in gobs in ditches and ponds, or gurgling from a few early rigs up in Pennsylvania. The embryonic automobile, too, with its clattering mess of an engine, still posed an unlikely threat to the horse.

For months, under the leadership of Higgins and his cadre of recruited engineers and sponsors, a team of drillers sank lengths of pipe into the soil without luck, fighting the subterranean nuisance of sand, clay, and rock, until on January 10 they noticed something strange. The level of mud in the pipe began to undulate. As quoted by authors Henry C. Dethloff and Robert W. McDaniel in their book *Pattillo Higgins and the Search for Texas Oil,* one of the drillers who'd worked on the well from its start, a twenty-four-year-old from Corsicana named Al Hamill, said "it was like the hole was breathing." At 1,139 feet deep, on the shoulders of an ancient salt-dome formation, the well had punctured a massive pocket of oil.

The hole let out a thunderous belch. Then it vomited something foul. The well ejected "a column of slime and blue gas" and a shower of thick, greasy mud, followed by the shrapnel of the well's own mechanical guts, six tons of pipes and equipment bursting from the site, splintering portions of the derrick's frail wooden lattice, sending the confused and terrorized men scrambling.

Then, for an eerie interval, *silence.*

Finally the oil came shooting up, a "solid stream of dirty green crude" that raged for more than a week, wasting between eighty thousand and a hundred thousand barrels a day before the crews managed to cap it with a T-valve mounted onto a sliding frame made of railroad track.

The most iconic image of the strike—you have surely seen it—was captured by photographer Frank Trost, who operated a studio in nearby Port Arthur and dashed to Beaumont with his equipment shortly after the thing blew.

Word of Spindletop, along with Trost's photograph, traveled quickly. Predicting the global shift it would trigger, the *New York Times* called it "A World Beater." The *Beaumont Journal* called it "too grand for intelligent description." Lore maintains that an unidentified worker on the well's site, striding past the plume moments after its eruption, simply called it a "gusher."

The latter stuck.

Within a year, starting as early as that afternoon's train, Beaumont's population ballooned from around nine thousand to over fifty thousand residents. A hasty boomtown was hammered up around the gusher, bringing with it the symptoms native to such rapid, haphazard expansion seen previously in states like California and Montana, with their respective rushes of gold and copper. Beaumont endured the growing pains associated with those booms of the recent past—the cases of trafficking and prostitution, oil fire after destructive oil fire, filthy and inadequate lodging, bureaucratic treachery over claims and property, the twinned hazards of liquor and violence, and on and on.

A hundred and eighteen years later, the museum orchestrates a reenactment of the strike a few times a month, geyser and all; only this time the well spits water, not oil. The production is powered by a three-hundred-horsepower behemoth of a pump that was salvaged from the U.S. government after a stint of service in the Persian Gulf, where it was used to smother the flames of wells ignited by Saddam Hussein's troops before their retreat. From a pipe that's plumbed directly to the city's main line, it takes forty-five minutes to fill the machine's three-thousand-gallon tank with fresh water. When the gusher blows with the same force it did in 1901, it will take only two minutes to empty it.

———

TWO WEEKS before attending the faux gusher's blastoff, in an attempt to gather some sense of perspective, I rode shotgun for several hours in the silver Ford Fusion of Juan Flores, weaving through the neighborhoods of Houston that bear the heaviest marks of a metropolis wholly dependent on oil. Juan serves as the community air monitoring program manager for Air Alliance Houston, an organization that collects and shares data on air quality and pollution levels throughout the city's eastside petrochemical corridor, where the Houston Ship Channel begins its muddy, port-lined trek toward the Intracoastal Waterway. He is the designated guide of Air Alliance's "toxic tours."

In his role as guide—a title he inherited by default, as one of the most road-savvy and gregarious in the organization—Juan leads groups of researchers, aspiring activists, and community members on educational ventures, showing them some of the area's most pressing environmental risks. The tour's route follows a jagged loop within the city, tracing the obscure perimeters of industrial sites. There is no clear objective, other than to observe, over and over, the bleak aesthetics of production and export. It's a morbid safari, and anyone is welcome to ride along.

Air Alliance's efforts deal particularly with the neighborhoods adjacent to or, in some cases, entirely surrounded by major refinement and processing facilities, places they've come to refer to as "fence-line communities." Neighborhoods like Manchester, portions of Pasadena, and the unincorporated township of Galena Park, where Juan grew up and still lives, hold the title of some of the most polluted residential blocks in the United States. A legacy of negligence among industrial facilities makes these areas reliably prone to toxic levels of emitted volatile organic compounds (VOCs), most notably benzene, a by-product of petrochemical processing, as well as various other gases and airborne particulates formed in all manner of chemical processes, from oil refinement to plastic making to metal recycling.

Residents here—primarily minority and immigrant families, many of whom work in the plants themselves—confront the lasting struggles typical of this proximity, suffering higher-than-average rates of cancer, asthma, and respiratory disease. They report offensive chemical odors, pervasive irritants of dust and haze, and unexplained explosions within close range of their houses. Some homeowners complain of cracked foundations caused by violent tremors emanating from nearby plants. Air Alliance reports approximately 484,000 pounds of toxic materials disperse each year throughout neighborhoods like Manchester and Galena Park, where their consequences abound, ranging from trivial to irreversible. Children develop mysterious coughs. Strange, dark, manmade clouds regularly float and park themselves over the residential zones. Cars wear heavy coats of chemical grime.

Still, the neighborhoods remain, and the corporations—some of them major names, like Valero, Goodyear, and LyondellBasell, but also smaller ones, one-off scrap recycling outfits that contribute their own toxic load just the same—keep closing in. Enabled in part by the city's absence of zoning regulations, facilities needn't heed precautions like buffer zones or residential–commercial building restrictions when setting up shop in poor communities. When it comes to the interests of capital and land use in Houston, anything goes. In some ways, this quirky trait of the nation's fourth most populous city can make it a welcoming and opportunity-rich place to live, backed by its impressive statistics on diversity and inclusion (Houston, for example, boasts one of the largest numbers of dialects spoken in one zip code, and has long been an affordable destination for the nation's highest concentrations of immigrants from Vietnam, Pakistan, and several other countries). Culture and architecture cross-pollinate in ways that aren't possible elsewhere, but this strain of hands-off city governance also promotes precarious, oppressive mashups of geography and commerce.

Historically, Juan told me, despite the threats faced by these neighborhoods, first-generation children of immigrants who built lives in Houston didn't flee. They stuck around. These neighborhoods are cultural touchstones that hold more significance than a structure and its address. They're generational landmarks, often the first landing spots for immigrants seeking familiar community—like Juan's Mexican-born parents once did—in an otherwise disorienting city and an increasingly intolerant federal immigration system. This rootedness rings especially true for elders, but with many in their generation now passing away, their children confront a harsh dilemma: Stay, dig in, and lock horns with the powers that be, or cut your losses, sell out for a meager price, and vacate to the city's cheaper, less-polluted outskirts? Most opt for the second strategy, causing the cultural networks of their childhood neighborhoods to shrink in size and spirit as they leave, a move Juan laments but also can't blame them for choosing.

"If you live here long enough," Juan said, alluding to the maddening cycle of industrial encroachment, coupled with the struggle to hold on to an inherited, meaningful space for families to grow, "you get to see it all."

It's exasperating, this tireless momentum of business and production and its disregard for the people living in the path of profit. Juan's and my struggle are not the same, but I empathize with him. Our experiences compare in shades nonetheless. When Juan saw the intensifying circumstance of his home's unsustainability, he chose to stay and act against it. My instinct, instead, bolstered by the entrenched confidence and apathy of American whiteness, was flight.

I asked Juan if there was a time, in a neighborhood's infancy perhaps, when people had a choice to be here or there, nestled with these businesses or farther out, seeking cleaner, less cramped environs.

"No way," he said. "We were here first, man. These refineries grew up around *us*. It wasn't the other way around."

In their early stages of development, those tracts of residential land next to new industrial property were sold as valuable, safe acres of opportunity. In fact, an early promotional pamphlet put out by the Magnolia Park Land Company in the 1920s cites the location as its chief selling point: "Right in the center of this tract is the land we have secured for Manchester Subdivision," the ad goes. "On all sides of it is industrial activity . . . The location of new plants will make still greater the demand for homes here, and the outlook is bright for a community of several hundred families with stores and shops, schools and churches and all the accessories of a thriving industrial city."

If you look at subsequent maps of Houston, following the correlations of land allotment and demographic shifts, you can see Manchester and Galena Park swallowed, slowly, as the institution of oil drilling in Texas matured toward the mid-twentieth century. The culprits were companies kickstarted by the very pocket of oil Pattillo Higgins allegedly had wandered over years earlier, witching stick in hand.

Only after the city's port grew busier, drawing in larger, unchecked industry, did these neighborhoods earn the undesirable reputation they bear today. By that point, the city's more mobile whites, finding this new atmosphere unsavory, exercised that privilege and abandoned the neighborhoods they'd once touted as the city's finest.

As in all cities, the story of displacement and discrimination is as old as the municipality's. While it might seem somewhat ahistorical to draw a direct, incriminating line from Spindletop's boom to the petroleum-reliant corporations that now dominate Houston and its high-risk neighborhoods, the weight of association is there. Houston, like every other metropolis, is guilty of the endemic environmental racism created by the very industry that paved the way for its growth. It's written into the city's code, embedded from day one in the city's naïve aspirations for its future.

The "toxic tour" with Juan Flores confronts these concerns directly, without diluting them with distance. At the wheel, his passion and fluency showed. Without the aid of map or notes, he spun a full narrative from nearly every home and street we passed. When Juan slowed the car and reached across my chest, for instance, he was pointing at the playground where his children spent much of their time, the same playground he grew up playing baseball and soccer in. The swings and seesaws set an idyllic, quaint scene, backed by a grass field and chain-link backstop. But when my gaze rose, a shocking tableau of machinery filled the frame, followed by a wall of smoke and steam erupting from the mess. The skyline of coughing smokestacks was all around us, their jagged peaks forming an irregular, rusted crown. Sitting there, I tried to imagine what it would be like to grow up without any glimpse of a natural horizon.

Juan kept driving, pointing out the homes of friends and

relatives, of strangers he'd gotten to know—for better or worse—through his work with Air Alliance. Several times a year, when the weather permitted, he conducted block walks, knocking on doors and taking surveys, informing neighbors of the environmental hazards their communities face, sharing Air Alliance's findings, and reminding residents of the rights and resources they could implement to help effect change.

Some are eager to talk, Juan said. They fill out questionnaires, hear the data, and seem grateful. Some aren't. Juan had been harassed by dogs (and followed, on one occasion, by a loose pig). He'd been met with his share of callous and indifferent responses. The previous year, while block-walking a whiter and more affluent quadrant of Pasadena, he had been threatened by a pair of men standing in their front yard, a large Confederate flag on full display in front of their house. He'd spun on his heels and left, quickening his steps.

Interrupting his own story, Juan abruptly stopped the car. "Look at this," he said. "This is ground zero." We were idling on a quiet street in Manchester, with Hartman Park and its community center to our left. To the right stood a small house, a modest bungalow sandwiched between two hulking white storage tanks, likely harboring crude oil or gasoline, on either side, plus another tank at its back, where a yard would be. Even in the late morning light, the tanks cast a full blanket of shade over the house.

Juan explained the mechanical function of these tanks, which I'd seen across Texas for my entire life, never fully understanding how they worked. The ones with the flat tops, he told me, are bad news. They operate with a "floating roof" that rides the level of fluid up and down as it fills and empties. During the flooding brought on by Hurricane Harvey, when the city was drenched in more than sixty inches of rain, most refineries and processing facilities shut down their monitoring systems, turning a blind eye to malfunctions. Instead of floating safely on top of their product, many of these tank lids couldn't withstand the weight of water above them and plunged, like a fist entering a bowl already filled with liquid, sending hazardous chemicals up and over the tanks' edges, into yards of neighboring houses and into the city's water supply. Assessing losses from the short period of the flood, facilities reported a combined total of more than eight million pounds of toxic material released into the air and water, an amount many believe to be an overly conservative estimate.

"During Harvey, out here the benzene levels were off the charts," Juan said. "You could smell it. It smelled like raw petrol. People were trying to leave Galena Park, but it's hard to leave when it's flooded in. You can't do nothin' but take it."

I wondered, silently, if Juan had considered leaving after the storm, if he'd ever been seduced by the notion of wiping his hands of the place, setting his principles aside. I wouldn't blame him if he had.

"My dad worked at a refinery," Juan said. "The one thing he always told me was 'Mijo, you make me happy, just don't work at a refinery like I am.'"

He never has. And neither have his siblings. But that doesn't mean his family is immune to the tragedies of oil.

Just a few years ago, Juan's daughter, his first biological child, was born with a tumor near her kidney. She underwent three rounds of chemotherapy before she was six months old. After Juan told me this, I asked—nervous I might come off as voyeuristic, or, worse, accusatory—if he felt like their family's decision to stay in Galena Park was at all responsible.

He sighed. He'd anticipated the question but didn't have an answer.

"I don't know, man," he said. "I don't know. But it's always in the back of my mind."

———

AT THE museum with Troy Gray, prior to the gusher reenactment, I'd learned a more condensed, yet similar, story of early Beaumont and its experience after the boom. In the winter of 1901, and for years after, not everyone considered the strike a blessing. The incessant drizzle of crude ruined surrounding crop fields and poisoned livestock. Lakes of oil formed around town, spreading outward from the wells until crews shoveled canals and levees to divert the flow. The paint on buildings was damaged by the omnipresent chemical mist.

Shortly before his death in 1955, Pattillo Higgins recalled this last phenomenon in an interview recorded by his son. "And the one thing I done for them Beaumonters," Higgins said, "I painted their houses, every one of them. Shining up big white buildings and such like. The gas, the sulfur in the air, kind of put a finish on the white paint—made it look *bronzy*."

Still waiting for the geyser's launch, I was killing time in the museum's gift shop, perusing the books Troy had recommended I purchase, when a woman working the cash register beckoned me over. There was a lull in her shift, and she wanted to chat. Her name was Jamie. I asked her how long she'd been working at the museum.

"Just a few months," Jamie said. Before that, she'd been in the Army. She'd served in Afghanistan for a tour, and after that she moved back to Vidor, a small town outside of

Beaumont. She used her GI Bill funds to start school down the road at Lamar University. Then Harvey hit. "I was at my house when the water came up," she said. "We had to get out."

Jamie was forced to walk twice through armpit-deep water to get to an evacuation boat, ferrying her two large bulldogs, one at a time, from her front door. On the second trip, carrying the heavier of the two, she felt an odd snag in her chest. She froze for a moment, then pushed through. Later that week, when she was finally able to see a doctor, she was told she'd suffered a severe heart attack. As if exposing a tender, buried secret, Jamie lifted an index finger to a point on her chest, just above the collar of her V-neck shirt, and traced the silver gash of a freshly healed scar.

"Triple bypass," she said, almost whispering.

A family of four entered the gift shop, signed the logbook, and began fingering the Texas-themed trinkets. One of the children, a boy of about eight, started flipping through one of the young-adult books about oil. The title was *The Night of Black Rain*.

After the family paid for their wares and left, Jamie told me how she'd lost her home, how she'd dropped out of school after the combined trauma of the flood and her surgery. She told me how by chance she'd stumbled upon one of the books sold at the museum, *Giant Under the Hill: A History of the Spindletop Oil Discovery*, and had fallen in love with the story of the origin of Gladys City, the town initially drawn up from Higgins's early aspirations for a Christianity-infused, wholesome, oil-boom utopia. Once he'd finished the plans, he'd named the proposed city after his prized Sunday school pupil, Gladys Bingham. Fascinated, Jamie had applied for the guest services job at Spindletop not long after the floodwaters receded in Beaumont. She liked it. She told me Troy even sometimes let her press the gusher's launch button, bolted on the gift shop's exterior wall.

Weeks before, I had asked the director of Air Alliance, Bakeya Nelson, "Should the city of Houston exist at all?" I wanted to know whether it made sense to her to keep fighting given events that emphasized the city's unsustainability. Bakeya quickly, confidently shot my question down.

"The question of whether or not it should exist is irrelevant," she said. "It exists, and so what do we do because it exists? How do we protect people? Because people live here."

———

TOWARD THE end of our "toxic tour" that day in Houston, Juan Flores wanted to me to see one last thing. He steered us in the direction of Buffalo Bayou, the city's arterial waterway that becomes—as it passes through downtown, widening to accept the tributaries of White Oak and Simms Bayou—one of the busiest deepwater ports on the continent. Approaching the water, we parked and made our way closer to the shore.

Juan told me he used to skip school and split a twelve-pack with friends at this spot on the bayou's banks, a city-owned patch of land between refineries where a squat stone plaque still stands, marking the location of Santa Anna's capture in 1836, following the Battle of San Jacinto. There, ducking out and relaxing on the small expanse of grass, Juan would watch the tankers and tugboats lurch past, carrying their products toward the Intracoastal Waterway. He didn't know it then, but he was forging a physical résumé for his future as an activist and organizer.

On the day we visited, the place was packed with fishermen, old men slouching on milk crates, drinking beer and spearing scraps of raw chicken onto their hooks, flinging their lines into the chop stirred up from barges. They were aiming to snag big cats, the channels and blues that patrol the deep holes of the bayous, and maybe a speckled trout or redfish or flounder, saltwater species that occasionally wandered into the bayou, fooled by the brackish tides.

"Look at that shit," Juan said. He pointed to the men, then swept his hand just a hundred yards upstream, where a house-sized island of trash bobbed, rotating slowly in the water, caught in a filthy eddy. "*That's* what scares me. Those people over there fishing!"

I balked slightly at Juan's quick condemnation of the fishermen. There were bigger concerns to be had, it seemed. And plus, maybe this was survival. Maybe, for some, those fish were better than nothing. It was a gorgeous, bright day, and it felt good to be outside and on foot after the tour's frenzied stop-and-go. The sun was dancing off the bayou, and Juan was pointing out the multitude of refinement companies lined along the opposite bank when I noticed, apropos of nothing, the jewelry hanging from his neck: a prominent silver chain laid over his shirt with what appeared to be a lizard, limbs splayed, climbing up his chest.

"It's a salamander with a pearl," he explained.

His wife had bought the necklace for him in Vegas at one of those places that farms the pearls on site, right there in front of you, and mounts them to any piece that strikes your fancy. For no real reason, briefly mesmerized, I fixated on the metallic, shimmering salamander, the jewel lodged in its tiny jaws.

All the dizzying talk of oil and gas had me tracing peculiar connections of the trade. The gleaming creature made from precious metal, dangling on Juan's chain. The sloshing tank of refined gasoline under his car (albeit a hybrid, assisted by electricity). The barges and their mountains of barrels hauling crude. The chocolate bayou surging through the city. The fish writhing in these men's hands, their aquatic stomachs ripe with trash, their veins laden with mercury. I wanted, and still strained, to see the city like Juan did, glowing with a potential worth investing in, but our tour had complicated that effort. I'd begun to build a kind of folk hero version of Juan in my head, but the ubiquity of his villain—the oil industry—grew more intimidating with every stop, working its way into my language, blurring my vision.

Just behind us, arching over the banks of the bayou, one man's fishing pole doubled over, the line taut and jerking. After a few minutes' fight, the fish, a sizeable black drum, was on land, and the man wrestled with it for a moment before removing the hook from its puckered mouth. Then, steadying it on the ground under his boot, he took a smooth rock and gave the fish one swift, efficient whack to the brain. He tossed it into a five-gallon bucket. Not twenty yards away, planted in the grass, a sign announced in English and in Spanish:

DANGER!
THE TEXAS DEPARTMENT OF STATE
HEALTH SERVICES HAS ISSUED A
SEAFOOD CONSUMPTION ADVISORY
FOR THIS WATER BODY DUE TO THE PRESENCE OF
TOXIC POLLUTANTS IN SEAFOOD!

Back at the Air Alliance headquarters, before parting ways, Juan led me into his office and showed me the alliance's next project. They were issuing residents home chemical-sampling kits. The device seemed simple enough—a plastic bucket with a one-way valve and an airtight bag inside. All you'd have to do, Juan explained, is open the valve, let the natural vacuum of the bag inhale a sample, seal it back up, and return it to Air Alliance for research. That way, residents could provide scientists with material taken immediately after anyone noticed strange odors or particulates in the air. It would put the process rightfully in the people's hands, the ones who are closest to the issue, the ones who live it daily. Juan's optimism at the prospect was clear, but I could also sense a weary skepticism in his trust of residents' participation.

Earlier on our drive, we'd passed his own house in Galena Park, and he'd spoken of the political complications there, his unsuccessful efforts to inspire action among his neighbors. In a bid for city council, he'd engaged in heated, unproductive debates with other candidates about development. "It got dirty," Juan said. One opponent had attempted to dazzle voters by promising to bring a Walmart to the neighborhood, which Juan had proved was unsound: the proposed site was on shifting, sandy soil dumped there during repeated dredgings of Buffalo Bayou and could not support safe construction. Subsequently, he told me, when he ran for mayor, his opponents fabricated accusations of a criminal history and claimed he'd lied about his daughter's medical condition to garner sympathy. Juan fought hard, canvassing and planting signs. Ultimately he lost to the incumbent candidate. Exhausted by the ordeal, he'd become disillusioned with hometown politics.

When I asked why he remained in Galena Park, a place he knew, maybe better than anyone else, was hazardous and difficult to love, his conviction returned. I could hear it hold firm in his voice. "We need to organize and fight, and educate," he told me. "If I leave, I'm part of the problem."

———

IN HER short, brilliant essay called "The Dart and the Drill," the writer Mary Ruefle interrogates the act of mining with haunting precision, beginning with an anecdote from her youth, then floating, associatively and poetically, through a survey of extraction in all its forms, from the primitive hunt for ore across generations and cultures, to the curious, probing instruments of NASA's Mars rover, to a hummingbird's needle-nosed beak rooting for nectar in a blossom, to the morbid image of a gold tooth attached to a necklace (an anniversary gift her father thought romantic but that was not received as such), to the gruesome medical act of trepanning, to the much softer, yet ultimately more devastating, tradition of psychological and emotional warfare. "The human brain seems to be obsessed with boring into other brains," Ruefle tells us, "and if none are available, one's own brain will do quite well," by which she means we are simply and hopelessly fated to fuck each other up, to forever pester and brood and sabotage ourselves and the ground we stand on. The essay offers no solution, winding instead to the infuriating conclusion that "no one has ever stopped trying, no one has ever stopped and said *Enough*, all these things do is make us shudder."

Years ago, when I first encountered Ruefle's essay, I was

stuck in a quicksand of depression, and I felt embraced and was brought to tears by Ruefle's words. I, too, had once bored into myself, taking the drill to my temple in figurative terms. In my junior year of high school, guilty by association with some wayward peers I hardly knew, I was accused of and detained for a crime I did not commit, a charge whose absurd particulars are too embarrassing even to mention now. In court, my parents lacked the funds or energy to fight the case, and my existing record of spotty attendance and slipping grades undermined my defense. Virtually stripped of choice, I pleaded *no contest* and accepted the conviction, a felony it turned out, and entered adulthood full of absolute rage—at myself, at the system that had produced me, at the dreariness of my prospects and surroundings.

In a flight of adventurous desperation, romanced by a recruiter in the cafeteria job fair, I enlisted in the Marine Corps as an infantry rifleman. During four years in the military, in Hawaii and on deployments in Iraq and Afghanistan, I lived in tents and mud huts with other young men, most of them Southern or Midwestern children of backgrounds astonishingly similar to my own, each of them harboring their own damaging inner fires. They became my brothers, and I still cherish the bonds we formed, but we unanimously bucked against military life, and when we completed our stints, we all eagerly took our discharge papers and dispersed. I found a new love in books and college, in writers I idolized and emulated. I was saved by the grace and generosity of intellectual mentors, and I eventually healed, given utmost purpose by the kindness of the woman who became my wife.

Occasionally, in correspondence or on social media, I catch up on the continuing lives of those friends I met in the

Marines. Many of them thrive in their new freedom, raising families and cultivating dreams, and many others have entered similarly extreme, military-adjacent fields of labor and travel, working as cops or security contractors. I see photos, too, of the large percentage of them who draw their paychecks from the oil and gas industry, their engagements strung out across the country, fixing pipe in obscure coordinates in North Dakota, or camped out in temporary trailer villages in West Texas, or serving rotating shifts out on rigs in the Gulf.

Some of them, finding the civilian world too large and wracked with dissonant noise, consider their lives useless and slide into steep trenches of mental illness. They spiral and flail in their silent, personal wars. Too many have lifted guns to their heads, and I mourn them still.

In my most thoughtful moments I want to reach out and wrap my friends up with time and patience, and love. At times I can and at others the responsibility overwhelms me. I'm absent and self-interested. My compassion fizzles.

———

AFTER MY tour with Juan Flores and my trip to Beaumont, I felt the need to go back and reread Mary Ruefle's essay. This time, coming to it with fresh eyes, in an older state of mind, it contained drastically new meaning. More than any charming aphorism, I now realized, it contained the gleaming possibility of promise, the option, or obligation, for someone, someday, to actually say *Enough*, to witness the patterns around them and change the narrative for good. It was a call to action, I now knew, not a passive rhetorical exercise.

I felt charged by this new impression, and I wanted to embody its message retroactively in support. In the same way I long to connect with the friends I see flailing, I wanted to reach out to Juan, assuring him that the work he was doing was right, was worth it. I wanted to tell Jamie, too. I wanted to cover them both in a protective shield of understanding, but all I could do was nod my head and listen.

———

FINALLY, BACK at Spindletop, with the countdown completed, Jamie triggers the gusher. Just as Troy promised, it unfurls into a forceful trajectory, straight up through the derrick's straddling beams and 125 feet beyond that, dwarfing the museum's campus. A mild wind has kicked up, and at the gusher's highest point it bends and plumes into a righteous fan, dissipating into the cloudy backdrop.

Along with the oil that day in 1901, other prehistoric debris was mixed in—stuff that had no business straying above bedrock. Shards of fossils, sediment imprinted with the shells of extinct crustaceans, buried deep for millennia until it fell like rain on the gusher's observers. A world inverted.

We catch no fossils in our palms. No ancient dust lands on our tongues. Instead, we stand on the asphalt, Troy and Jamie before us, proud keepers of their fountain, the symbolic tick mark on the timeline of our bumbling tribe of humans, when we unlocked some deep, treacherous code of the planet, a curse we could never stuff back into the box from which it came.

Eventually, the gusher exhausts its supply and disappears. Troy and Jamie head back inside. The rest of us load into our cars and leave, splintering into our respective headings home.

On the road, I point the car toward Houston. I'm staying at my mother's house tonight, as I usually do when I'm in town, sleeping in a small bed among her vast family of cats. I'll be back there by the evening, but I'm in no hurry, so I take the side roads into the city, navigating intuitively, stopping here and there for coffee and gas. At one point, a little lost, feeling inexplicably glum, I get out and stand beside the car, listening, waiting for nothing in particular. I'm parked on a gravel road next to a clearing in a field of tall grass and mesquite, where an oil pumpjack nods, thumping out its faint cadence. I get back in the car and keep going, winding at last through the labyrinthine suburbs. Nearing downtown, I can see the concentrated silhouette of tanks and refineries, the smokestacks all in a line, their familiar curls of white and yellow steam. It looks like the city is breathing.

ACKNOWLEDGMENTS

This project began at the University of Montana, in Missoula, when I did not believe I had a book in me. Thanks, forever, to the mentors and friends who did. Among them are Walter Kirn, Amanda Fortini, Bryan Di Salvatore, Robert Stubblefield, Judy Blunt, Deirdre McNamer, Debra Magpie Earling, Kevin Canty, David Gates, and many others.

The three years I spent as a graduate student at the University of Iowa's Nonfiction Writing Program changed my life and opened my mind to the possibilities of the genre. I am incredibly grateful for the brilliant, compassionate, and generous people I came to know there, as well as the rare gift of time and space to work I received through the Iowa Arts Fellowship. I could not have completed this book without the support and wisdom of my NWP cohort of Brittany Borghi, Dylan Cooley, Taney Kurth, Emily Mester, Robert Peck, Dina Peone, Katie Prout, and Lucy Schiller. Extra support from my dear friends Landon Bates and Max Rubin kept me sane, laughing, and motivated. Sincere thanks to past and present faculty members John D'Agata, Kerry Howley, Jeff Porter, Inara Verzemnieks, Patricia Foster, and Bonnie Sunstein.

I also wish to thank the Iowa City Parks and Recreation Department for employing me as a trash collector in the summers of 2016, 2017, and 2018. I wrote much of this book in my head while driving a truck full of dog feces through the beautiful parks of that town.

This book was sustained in part by the *Oxford American* magazine's Jeff Baskin Writers Fellowship, awarded in honor of the late Jeff Baskin, a passionate librarian and ambassador of the literary arts in Central Arkansas. My time in Arkansas afforded me the freedom to think and write alongside an inspiring team of editors and writers dedicated to celebrating the complexity and vitality of the American South through original storytelling. I was fortunate enough to share the early vision of this book in the pages of the *Oxford American*, and I extend special thanks to past and present staff members Eliza Borné, Maxwell George, Ryan Harris, Jay Jennings, Sara A. Lewis, Hannah Saulters, and many others.

My outstanding agent, Lauren Sharp, led me confidently and calmly through the unfamiliar landscape of the publishing industry. She trusted and challenged me, and her insight and optimism kept this book alive. Editors Alane Mason and Mo Crist put in the painstaking, invisible labor to give these pages shape and story. They and many others at W. W. Norton worked hard to make the object in your hands a reality.

Acknowledgments

Annabelle, my dog, was a constant muse and friend under the desk, on hikes, and in the boat when I needed to cool the tubes after writing.

Finally, I wish to thank my partner, Amanda, for her continued sacrifice in service to this book and my writing life. She is a model of grit, dedication, and love. I owe her it all.

A NOTE ON SOURCES

We Hold Our Breath was born from over a decade of on-the-ground interviews, observations, photographs, late-night conversations, long walks, meditative drives, internet wandering, and traditional, in-the-stacks research. A great number of written sources informed the historical facts and critical perspective of this book, but the driving inspiration for this project was the physical object of Houston itself, the people that live there, and the ephemera of that world. It is impossible to cite all that here. A constant guide in my creative life is the writer James Agee, particularly his masterpiece of nonfiction, *Let Us Now Praise Famous Men*, a lyrical exploration of the lives of sharecroppers in the American South accompanied by the striking photography of Walker Evans.

In the book, Agee reflects on the exasperating limitations of documentary writing:

> *If I could do it, I'd do no writing at all here. It would be photographs; the rest would be fragments of cloth, bits of cotton, lumps of earth, records of speech, pieces of wood and iron, phials of odors, plates of food and excrement.*